CERC Monograph Series in Comparative and
International Education and Development No. 6

The Lending Power of PISA:
League Tables and Best Practice in International Education

Eduardo Andere

Comparative Education Research Centre
The University of Hong Kong

First published 2008
Comparative Education Research Centre
Faculty of Education
The University of Hong Kong
Pokfulam Road, Hong Kong, China

ISBN 978 988 17852 1 3

Series Editor: **Mark Mason**
Production Editor: **Emily Mang**

Cover design: Eduardo Andere, Susana Cuéllar and Vincent Lee
Cover photographs: Eduardo Andere

Contents

List of Abbreviations and Acronyms

ACT	Australian Capital Territory
ANMEB	Acuerdo Nacional para la Modernización de la Educación Básica
ANT	Actor Network Theory
BLTT	borrowing, lending, translating and transferring
CER	*Comparative Education Review*
CWEC	Common World Educational Culture
DMES	Decision Making in Education Systems
EPS	Edmonton Public School System
F&Q	Factors and Quality
GSEA	Globally Structured Educational Agenda
ICCR	International Center for Classroom Research
IEA	International Association for the Evaluation of Educational Achievement
IFAI	Instituto Federal de Acceso a la Información Pública
IMF	International Monetary Fund
ISTOF	International System for Teacher Observation and Feedback
LLECE	Latin American Laboratory for Assessment of the Quality of Education
NCLBA	No Child Left Behind Act
NY	New York
OECD	Organisation for Economic Co-operation and Development
OREALC	UNESCO's Regional Office for Latin America and the Caribbean
PIRLS	Progress in International Reading Literacy Study
PISA	Programme for International Student Assessment
SACMEQ	Southern and Eastern African Consortium for Monitoring Educational Quality
SBM	site- or school-based management
SNTE	Sindicato Nacional de Trabajadores de la Educación
TIMSS	Trends in International Mathematics and Science Study

List of Tables

List of Figures

Acknowledgments

Many people and organizations were involved in my project. I appreciate the support from my home university *Instituto Tecnológico Autónomo de México* (www.itam.mx), the Mexican National Science and Technology Council (www.conacyt.mx), the Mexican Foundation for Education Technology and Science (www.funed.mx), and from the following people who encouraged or supported me to continue with this long project: Arturo Fernández, Rafael Fernández de Castro, Francisco Gil, Lorenzo Servitje and Carlos Rojas Mota Velasco. Special thanks to George Flowers, an extraordinary human being, who tirelessly read and corrected the longer draft manuscript of the project for an English edition. Thanks also to Mark Mason and Mark Bray who first hosted me during my visits to Hong Kong schools under the aegis of the Hong Kong University Faculty of Education and the Comparative Education Research Centre (CERC). Mark Mason not only encouraged me to continue, but spent a good deal of time reading and suggesting changes to the manuscript. Also at CERC, Emily Mang and, at a later stage, Kokila Roy Katyal invested time reviewing or making sure the project was finally published. Jouni Välijärvi from Jyväskylä University was of fundamental help right from the beginning. Many people helped me worldwide and I mention a few with whom I have forged a lasting friendship. In Finland, Maarit and Jukka Rossi, Pirjo Lynnakylä, and Hannele Niemi. In France at the OECD, Andreas Schleicher, Barry McGaw, Gregory Wurzburg, Patricia Comte, Gérard Bonnet and Denis Meuret. Angélica Careaga and Leticia Chávez from the British Council in Mexico City, and Mathew Knowles from the British Council in Edinburgh. The British Council not only supported me with partial funding, but also in organizing school visits. In the UK, Audrey Brown, Isobel McGregor, Susan Robertson, Roger Dale and Michael Crossley. In Flanders, Gaby Hostens, Walter and Anita Roggeman and Kaat Vandensavel. In the Czech Republic, Ms. Undragova and Jana Korbelová. In Switzerland, Robert and Hilda Burch, Lutz Ortel, Otto Hutter and Ursula Mathez. In Singapore, Allan Luke, Saravanan Gopinathan, David John Hogan, Hwei Ming Wong, Yuyun Wirawati and Nicholas Tang, all from the Centre for Research in Pedagogy and Practice of the National Institute of Education. In Australia, Wendy Whithman, George Flowers, and Gordon and Trish Dowd. In New Zealand, Robyn Baker, Cathy Wylie,

Garry Cooper, Jane Gilbert, Rachel Dingle and Marie Cameron, all from the New Zealand Council for Educational Research. In South Korea, Mee-Kyeong Lee from the Korean Institute of Curriculum and Evaluation, and Agatha Yoo. In Japan, Hiroshi Omura from the Ministry of Education. In the United States of America Chris Coxon, Barbara Connoly, Diane Ravitch and Mary Brabeck, the Dean of the Steinhardt School of Education at NYU. I appreciate the comments of Gita Steiner-Khamsi on an earlier draft. In Canada, Diane Viel, Patrice Laffleur, Waldemar Riemer and Emilie DeCorby. In Chile, Ema Lagos, Lorena Meckes and Guillermo García, all from SIMCE. I thank also the team of English editors, Judy Elliot, Gerard Norris and Rose Malinaric for their professional work. In Mexico the list is long and a detailed acknowledgment has been written in the narrative version of my project.* Special thanks to Alejandro Caballero, Helga Luna Munguía and Susana Cuéllar for assisting in data organizing and data description. Susy has endured a long and demanding project with faithful, indefatigable and professional work. Finally, my gratitude goes to all principals, teachers and experts, who kindly opened their schools, classrooms or offices for a long survey.

---

*Andere, M. Eduardo. 2007. *¿Cómo es la mejor educación en el mundo? Políticas Educativas y Escuelas en 19 Países.* [*How Does it Look, the Best Education in the World? Education Policies and Schools in 19 Countries*]. Mexico DF: Editorial Santillana.

Series Editor's Foreword

The Programme for International Student Assessment (PISA) is a project of the Organisation for Economic Co-operation and Development (OECD), designed to provide policy-oriented international indicators of the skills and knowledge of 15-year-old students. PISA introduces itself thus:

Are students well prepared for future challenges? Can they analyse, reason and communicate effectively? Do they have the capacity to continue learning throughout life? The OECD Programme for International Student Assessment (PISA) answers these questions and more, through its surveys of 15-year-olds in the principal industrialised countries. Every three years, it assesses how far students near the end of compulsory education have acquired some of the knowledge and skills essential for full participation in society.

However, in their recent volume, *PISA According to PISA: Does PISA Keep What It Promises?*, Hopmann *et al.* (2007) suggest that PISA tends to treat the links between student, school and national achievement as self-evident, an approach which all too easily lends itself to a black-box theory of schooling where the more than occasionally arbitrary coincidence of particular factors with particular results is set down into correlations and causalities, without much accounting for these relationships. They suggest that while PISA and the national testing it inspires address only a few aspects of schooling, largely ignoring the relationships between the structure of schooling and social class and diversity within the broader society, its findings are produced as 'evidence' in ongoing debates in which failing schools and teachers are viewed as primarily responsible for the uneven distribution of knowledge and cultural capital in Western societies. Further, they suggest that although PISA uses advanced statistical tools, methodologically the programme reflects a pre-Popperian positivism that takes item responses for the realities towards which they gesture. There is, suggest Hopmann *et al.*, no theory of schooling or of the curriculum here that might make space for a non-affirmative stance towards the policy-driven expectations which, according to the OECD, 'determine' the design of PISA and the format in which its findings are reported.

Accordingly, questions about situatedness, multi-perspectivity, non-linearity or the contingency of social action are largely absent in PISA's design. Of course, admit Hopmann *et al.*, incorporating such contingencies on such a large scale would be close to impossible: and they do not, after all, lend themselves to such generalized bottom-lines as league tables. For Hopmann *et al.*, the risk in all this lies in the extent to which PISA's 'methodological reductionism' will prevail as the state of the art in comparative education research. More urgently, what will be the long-term effect of its conceptualization of student achievement on the public's understanding of what schooling is about? What will happen, they ask, to the school subjects left out, to the special needs that are marginalized, to school tasks which have nothing to do with higher-order academic achievement, to school functions that lie beyond a one-dimensional kind of knowledge distribution? In our entering an emerging age of accountability, both marked and assisted by the likes of PISA, we are at risk, they suggest, of leaving behind our social conscience if in our approaches to research, policy and schooling we march too closely to PISA's drum.

In similar vein, Eduardo Andere suggests in this book that the 'lending power' of international studies such as PISA is limited. PISA might be a good instrument for measuring and comparing some educational inputs and outputs but, suggests Andere, this is not enough for translation across contexts. He finds that PISA is not a very powerful instrument for explaining causal relationships in educational achievement, and nor for making claims about models or directions of education systems across the world. Basing his arguments on a qualitative study in 19 countries around the world and on a review of the centralization/decentralization and policy borrowing/lending literatures, Andere presents some of the conflicting evidence about the different meanings of education policies and ideas in different contexts. He suggests that it is problematic to compare policies, processes and practices across the different contexts of school education, thus rendering transferability across educational jurisdictions even more challenging. To understand the reasons behind performance or underperformance in school education, we have to construct, he concludes, a coherent narrative of a particular school and of the model of education in which the school is embedded.

As Michael Crossley has frequently cautioned, context matters. For these reasons, I welcome this volume into the *CERC Monograph Series in Comparative and International Education and Development*. It offers a timely and valuable critique of an area that currently commands a lot of attention in the field of comparative education research.

Mark MASON

Editor
CERC Monograph Series in Comparative and
International Education and Development

Director
Comparative Education Research Centre
The University of Hong Kong

References

Hopmann, S. T., Brinek, G., and Retzl, M. (Eds.) (2007) *PISA According to PISA: Does PISA Keep What It Promises* (Vienna and Berlin: Lit Verlag).

Introduction

The demand for international studies such as the Programme for International Student Assessment (PISA) seems to be growing. From a start of around 40 participating countries in PISA 2000 and 2003, PISA 2006 had 57 countries, while 62 countries are signed up for PISA 2009. Using the PISA studies as a backdrop, this monograph investigates the reasons behind the many difficulties before policies and practices can travel across countries and systems of school education. Thus, based on a non-representative survey of experts and schools, I try to delineate the limitations of the lending power of PISA.

The Field Trip and Findings
In my qualitative search for best policies and practices in schools I decided to conduct fieldwork as I wanted to collect data and information that was more in-depth and revealing than what was available from existing statistical data only. My focus was in gathering qualitative data from surveys and interviews with people who were actively involved in their own education systems. In order to achieve this I traveled extensively, and visited schools and met experts in high-performing countries as I wanted to establish, on a case-by-case basis, the meaning of policies and practices in school education systems in a variety of countries. I realized at the outset that the project would require a great deal of personal involvement and commitment. My active personal involvement in the study would have a further benefit as data gathered by a single researcher would ensure homogeneity in the methodology and practices of gathering and construing data. With a draft proposal in hand, I mapped out an agenda and this set in motion a flurry of activity. I had to deal with thousands of e-mails, phone calls and letters, and devote hours of work before I was able to finalize an agenda and itinerary that would give me access to schools and offices of education experts.

The outcome of this study is somewhat different from other international studies – alternative and complementary interpretations were arrived at that differed from those reached by international organizations such as the Organisation for Economic Co-operation and Development (OECD), though in many ways this story is neither better nor worse than the OECD's. I looked for evidence to support or refute the proposition of 'best practices' in school education policies and systems, believing that, if I could identify the best practices, then I would be able to add evidence to the hypothesis of convergence in school education policies and systems, and to the view of a world with declining national

1

power or influence over school education policies and practices. With the advantage of hindsight I can now emphasize that the concept of best practices in school policy is a myth, albeit a very good one. PISA shows significant differences in performance among countries. The results highlighted Mexico as the country with the lowest performance level among the OECD's countries. If Mexico is indeed lagging in student performance, what then can be said about its performance at the level of policies, processes and systems of education? Are the OECD's claims about best practices from the PISA findings true? (See, for instance, Guichard 2005; OECD 2005a; OECD 2005b; OECD 2006; Schleicher 2005, 2006a and 2006b.) Or are conclusions from PISA and other international studies (such as Trends in International Mathematics and Science Study (TIMSS) and the Progress in International Reading Literacy Study (PIRLS) faulty enough as to limit the nature of comparisons and translation of inputs, outcomes, policies and practices? PISA itself has been questioned on technical grounds (Bonnet 2002; Goldstein 2004a, 2004b; Prais 2003). Regardless of the technical (or lack of technical) merits of PISA, my research seems to show that there are other difficulties in the construction of PISA assessments that need to be investigated before we can translate the lessons into effective policies and practices across the world.

Even using powerful software and modern techniques for multivariate analysis, the issues are so complex that statistical techniques tell us very little about the real-world correlations and even less about variables marrying cause to effect. This is because PISA and other international studies need significantly greater fragmentation of samples to account for differences in schools and systems in order to make claims about what works and what does not. In reality, given the different meanings of concepts and features of education systems, it is possible that sampling cannot be done for aspects such as a simple comparison of compulsory education systems:

> Because of differences within and across countries in what *compulsory schooling* means, we conclude that goal is probably impossible to achieve. (Porter & Gamoran 2002, p.10)

The goal referred to is an estimate of achievement in the final year of compulsory education. Different education policies and ideas (such as decentralization, school autonomy, compulsory education, curriculum implementation, etc.) mean different things to different people. Thus, it seems logical to assume that there are some issues that are difficult to frame for sampling and comparison. Consequently, I intended to contribute some qualitative evidence to the view that, when it comes to policies, processes and practices, it is extremely problematic to compare the different worlds of school education, thus rendering the concept of transferability even more challenging.

Of course, comparisons can be made for certain inputs and outputs (as shown in Table 5.1). However, at the level of policies, processes and practices, this is not always possible. Claims about causal relationships such as best practices are easier to make than substantiate.

Furthermore, the different characteristics of sampled observations require more detailed fragmentation or stratification. Breaking down schools into clusters with similar characteristics needs to be done to the finest detail so as to account for the almost unaccountable combinations of school types, characteristics and arrangements (see summary in Table 5.2 and elsewhere in this book). This fragmentation needs to be minutely detailed as researchers are increasingly required to fragment their observation units into many clusters. I would argue that the holistic ('amass-it-all') type of research, where education is viewed in its entirety, must be fragmented into smaller parts. However, once the fragmentation enables the researcher to observe the 'real life' of school education systems and interactions between authorities and schools, teachers, students and families, it is possible to design a case-by-case method of analysis of systems and schools. This breakdown is necessary if an understanding of the whys and wherefores of school education policies and practices is to be reached. Without this understanding, a holistic approach can confuse rather than clarify matters, especially if the goal is to shed light on which paths to follow in school education policies and practices. If the objective is just to compare outcomes such as PISA results, international studies may have seemingly sound interpretations (Porter & Gamoran 2002). But even before PISA, some researchers were reluctant to accept the comparative validity of international studies claiming that international studies do not focus on "within-country" factors that affect performance (Theisen et al 1986).

Given the observed variety and complex interactions of schools, classrooms and models of school education policies and practices in places around the world (Table 5.2), there is no way that we can have a fully appropriate sample size. To explain the whys, hows, whats, for whoms and wherefores—i.e. causal relationships—we would need to investigate thoroughly those specific case-by-case units of analysis. These units are specific to the characteristics of school systems and schools, and the samples would need to be as stratified as necessary to reflect a situation comprising as many layers as there are schools. Eventually what is left is case-specific analyses, where the appropriate method of inquiry is only possible with narratives (Bruner 1996, and also Czarniawska 1998). Thus, to understand the reasons behind performance or underperformance in school education we have to construct a 'story' of the school and the model of education in which the school is embedded. The importance of a specific context is why many principals, teachers and experts around the world reject the idea of comparing schools in league tables (ranking tables).

Though PISA is an excellent instrument for measuring and comparing some inputs and outputs or just plain standardized performance on an overall basis, this is not enough. PISA is not a very powerful instrument for explaining causal relationships, or for making claims about models or directions of systems across the world. From the findings of this study it becomes overwhelmingly clear that policies, processes and practices in school education based on PISA do not seem to be transferable or able to 'travel.'

Best-practice Model
The comparison of outcomes may provide, at best, some measure of performance of policies and practices as they have been designed and implemented in the past. Policy-makers may link high performance to 'successful' policies and practices and low performance to unknown factors. However, if some best policies and practices could be identified in these high-performing countries, then countries exhibiting deficiencies could import or borrow policies and practices from high performers.

In order to reach higher levels of performance, one simply needs to look at the patterns or tendencies in policies, processes and practices of high-performing countries and borrow their recipes for success. Borrowing in this fashion – traveling around the world in search of best practices – is not new. The many attempts that developed and developing countries make to search for best practices is documented by the relatively recent but increasing body of literature on borrowing and lending. The literature also documents the failure of borrowing, lending, translating and transferring (BLTT) policies and practices. Some attempts have been made to develop general propositions for BLTT (O'Neill 1995, Popkewitz 1996, Lindblad & Popkewitz 2004a, 2004b, Schriewer & Martínez 2004, Phillips 1989, Steiner-Khamsi 2004 and Steiner-Khamsi & Stolpe 2004). Consequently, there appears to be a case for this epistemic group to cross-fertilize with a totally different group doing similar research from a different perspective, such as sociology of associations and organizations (Actor Network Theory – ANT) as will be seen later.

Based on PISA and related research and analysis, the OECD has benchmarked a model of best practices, and the focus of this study was to test the lending power of a school education best practices model across many countries. Questions addressed to experts or practitioners from "high performing countries" elicited responses from people who participate in or are knowledgeable about those countries or regions. In the OECD's model, they represent best-practice systems. By interviewing and surveying many representatives from best-practice countries or systems, I endeavored to obtain perceptions about practices that worked and those that did not. I believed that, should I obtain similar answers from all of them, then this would be evidence of a world of education that looks increasingly similar. However, if the responses were different, even from this non-representative group of knowledgeable people, the construction placed on the findings would be quite different. It would then be difficult to claim that there is a general convergence and that there is the possibility of a 'best practice' model that could be followed in school education. In other words, the reality of the world of schools could possibly be explained by a model that does not conform to one representing converging cultures of educational postulates.

A world culture model or convergence theory (Boli et al 1985; McNeely & Cha 1994; McNeely 1995; Kamens et al 1996; Meyer et al 1997; Baker & LeTendre 2005) of comparative education policies would buttress the PISA lending power by maintaining that some values that are intrinsic in nature promote convergence to a single identifiable structure or shape of school education model. For example, more as opposed to less decentralization of decision-making, devolution of power to schools, on-site management of schools (autonomy), curriculum isomorphism, mass schooling, etc. If these patterns really exist, they should be consistently and significantly similar across systems.

My research, however, arrives at a different conclusion. There are convergences as suggested by the convergence or isomorphistic theorists. However, convergence occurs only with some inputs and outputs. Policies, which in themselves are understood as processes or production functions of education, have not converged; nor do they seem to be converging. One conclusion from this research is that while international studies and international organizations can compare inputs (enrolment levels and rates, curriculum topics and contents, financial resources, school resources, etc.) and some outcomes (enrolment, performance based on standardized tests), they cannot make claims about the consistent relationship between policies and process and outcomes or performance. Nor can they establish a causal relationship between inputs, policies and outcomes that applies to all systems.

The Story of the Field Research

So, I did my chores, packed my things and went in search of the global model of school education. As a direct result of the conclusions and suggestions of PISA and TIMSS, I had in my mind a set of pre-conceptions. These centered primarily on what works and does not work in school education policies and practices. Armed with a supply of statistically driven deductive findings, I ventured out into the inductive world of school education in search of best practices. My objective was to test the lending power of PISA, with a view to finding a best practice model – and I built a data set comprising qualitative information gathered from numerous questionnaires and interviews with experts (academic and government) and professionals (principals and teachers) from schools in high-performing countries in order to fulfill my aims. However, as my travels proceeded, the reality of the task proved more complicated and arduous than I had envisaged. It took more than eighteen months to gather and compile all the data from the 165 schools and 565 questionnaires from the 19 countries involved. It took another year to condense and prepare the data for reporting.

I commenced my global journey as a metaphorical Marc-Antoine Jullien and ended up as Michael Sadler.[1] I decided to show the results as they actually occurred, comparing them with the results of the pre-conceived best practice model. I compared and contrasted two different world views in school education: convergence and divergence.

Hundreds of researchers before me have studied the field for years and have come up with alternative explanations for the way things seem to happen in the real world. My almost three-year-long research followed a theoretical road of epistemic travels. This included first looking at the meta analysis – a World-Bank, OECD-like approach. Since I was testing the lending power of league table studies, I resorted to a narrative approach in an attempt to establish not the workability of one model over others, but the circumstances and context in which a specific model may work or not, thus echoing Dale[2] who said, the real question is: "Work for whom and how and under what circumstances?"

---

[1] In an informal conversation with Prof. Michael Crossley in his office at the University of Bristol on June 6, 2006, when I was verbally relating my story, Michael interrupted me and said something like the following: 'In a way, you are paraphrasing the interaction between the founding fathers of comparative education: Jullien in search of the ideal model studied and systematized information of education systems; fifty years later Sadler, in his famous 1900 speech, warned us about the limits of traveling tales and traveling policies.'

[2] Personal interview on June 7, 2006 in Prof. Roger Dale's office.

Selection of Countries and the Gathering of Data

A high-performing country from an education point of view might be defined in various ways. In order to restrict this definition I decided to use students' results from international standardized assessments and from all the available assessments I selected PISA 2000/2002 and PISA 2003. A high-performing country according to PISA is a country, region or system that performs at or above the average or mean score value in either of the two assessments (i.e., PISA 2000/2002 and PISA 2003) once the equivalent areas of assessment (in reading, mathematics and science) from the first two rounds of PISA are taken into consideration. Thus, all of the high-performing countries lie above the mean value of 1,419 for PISA 2000/2002 or above 1,454 for PISA 2003[3]. The final selection of countries within that criterion was based on willingness on the part of the schools to accommodate my proposed visit. Most of the countries contacted accepted my incursion.

Quest for a Unit of Analysis

During the design of my research and while I was implementing my fieldwork, I grappled with the issue of the right unit of analysis. The questions to be asked during my survey and interviews could not be addressed properly by looking only at the aggregate national or federal or country-wide unit of analysis. I had to frame and reframe the questions and the answers at the regional or district level of analysis to make sense. For many of the questions the state, provincial or local district perspective was more appropriate than the federal or national one. I decided to focus on regions within countries and this brought the number of observed education systems to 28. This is the chronological order in which visits and interviews took place in the following systems: Finland, Sweden, France, England, Scotland, Ireland, Flanders, Wallonia (two observations only), the Czech Republic, Switzerland (17 observations in German cantons and four observations in French cantons), Singapore[4] (not a PISA country and only five observations from academics), New South Wales, the Australian Capital Territory, New Zealand (Wellington), Hong Kong, South Korea (Seoul), Japan

---

[3] The mean value for PISA 2003 was calculated from the aggregated mean for each country of three assessments only (reading, mathematics and science). To facilitate comparison between the first two rounds of PISA, the fourth area of assessment (problem solving) was not included.

[4] Singapore, a non-PISA country, was included in the sample since Singapore is the highest performing country in TIMSS. In TIMSS 2003 (Mullis et al 2004, pp.34-35) Singapore ranked first above all sampled countries assessed for 4th and 8th grades. Only five interviews were conducted in Singapore.

(Tokyo), Boston, New York City, Quebec City, Montreal, Alberta (Edmonton), British Columbia (Vancouver, three observations only), Mexico (Mexico City – DF, the State of Mexico, and Aguascalientes), and Chile (Santiago de Chile).

Of the above countries, states or regions, I treat Mexico as a single unit except where otherwise noted. Mexico has a fairly centralized education system. I have merged the three observed entities into a single unit labeled Mexico. The same applies to Belgium. The analysis and interpretation of data applies only to Flanders, unless otherwise noted. Another difficult unit to aggregate was that of Britain (referred to as UK[5] in OECD publications). Even though the OECD publishes only aggregated data[6] on the UK, I treated England and Scotland, as separate regions or countries.

The three most difficult countries to separate into component parts for the purpose of analysis were Canada, the US and Switzerland. The districts I selected for visiting were based on personal judgment, convenience and availability. For the remainder of the countries I tried to visit schools in the capital or surrounding cities or areas. At first, I tried the same approach for Canada, the US and Switzerland. However, even after several personal appeals to the federal authorities in Washington DC, there was no definite response. In the end, I decided to visit schools in the New York City and Boston districts, where my request met with a positive response.

The breakdown of my sample into smaller units reduced the size of the number of observations by the units of analysis from each country. From the outset I knew that at least one person from each of the following clusters would be personally interviewed: principals, teachers, government experts or policy-makers and academics. The total number of observations or people actually interviewed or surveyed amounted to 565. The total number of observations excluding low-performing countries (Chile and Mexico) amounted to 473. In the end, many more observations than one per cluster were finally secured as can be seen in Annex.

Sample: Hurdles and Limitations
Schools and experts to be interviewed were not selected by a random-

---

[5] Since the four countries of the United Kingdom of Great Britain, (England, Scotland, Wales and Northern Ireland) were included in PISA studies.

[6] In Annexes A and B of PISA results (OECD 2004, pp.305-471) some data is shown for regions or countries within national entities such as Scotland, Wales and Northern Ireland, and the Flemish and French Communities in Belgium for example.

based method since, with very limited resources, it was impossible to do research in this way. The project design required a single researcher to ensure homogeneity in the construction and analysis of data sets. In addition, without the support of international organizations such as the OECD, UNESCO or the World Bank, with access to government authorities to facilitate lists of schools and access to schools, random studies would be impossible. Even with access to homogenous lists of high-performing schools, the task would not be possible. In some countries it is illegal to produce league tables of national or international examinations. In others it is politically incorrect even to request the lists.

In best practice analysis based on perceptions of a non-randomized survey, there are always limitations to the scope and strength of conclusions and recommendations. Conclusions have to be limited, strictly speaking, to the group of people and schools surveyed. On this basis, statistical inferences about school districts cannot be made. Having said that however, since special care was taken in the selection of schools and only one researcher conducted all the interviews and visits to schools, I am confident of the appropriateness of the answers as a reflection of reality in the schools.

Therefore, since the countries, districts or regions I have chosen are included among the high-performing countries, it is not too much of a stretch to say that they reflect the policies and trends (or the lack of them) in countries with high levels of student performance.

The Conducting of Interviews and Observations
The first problem to be faced was that of definitions. The second challenge was a rejection by most people interviewed of classifying countries in a league-table fashion. League tables, as I was told by many interviewees, do not convey information about what is going on inside the education systems or the schools. To talk about best practices in education and school policies and practices is therefore inaccurate and misleading. After a few weeks of conducting interviews and surveys, I decided to change the title of my project from "Best practices in policies and practices of highest-performing countries" to "Good education policies and practices in highest-performing countries." This was not enough. A few weeks later, having conducted dozens more interviews, I decided to downscale once again to "Good education policies and practices in high-performing countries." With this more modest title I continued my interviews and visits.

The first lesson is that there are no best practices and no highest-performing countries. As I have stated before, international studies can tell us in a ranking order the distance between high performers and low performers. They cannot tell us:

- The comparability of assessed students (they may be 15-year-old students, but that does not mean that these students have been subjected to similar experiences);
- The causality between inputs and outputs, or between policies and processes and outputs, at least not consistently across systems;
- The predictability of inputs and processes in relation to outcomes and results;
- The transferability of policies, processes and practices with the same meaning.

Another problem that I encountered during my visits and interviews, perhaps more acutely than I had expected, was in the definition of some concepts and expressions. I found that many of my questions were culturally driven by my own background and that of education systems more familiar to me, namely those of Mexico and the US. I had difficulty in explaining the concepts of centralization, devolution of power, governance and autonomy. These concepts offer significant latitude in interpretation, as will be shown later. Many of my interviewees were uncomfortable with the words decentralization and centralization. This leads me to believe that the meaning of those words is both culturally and context driven.

Culture and Context
The prospective respondents were asked the following question about centralization of education system and policy: How centralized is the education policy in your country? This led to the first problem in inter-pretation. For very centralized, monolithic systems the answer is very straightforward. However, for decentralized systems like those in the US, Australia, Canada and Switzerland or even the UK and Belgium, the answer is less clear and also complicated.

Participants were asked the question from the perspective of the overall system, from the national or federal point of view. But they were also given the opportunity to elaborate, especially when their system is fragmentized. Some of the respondents went so far as to provide two answers: one for the country-wide perspective and one for the frag-mentized unit, for example Boston in relation to the U.S, or Flanders in relation to Belgium. To such elaborations I finally decided to mark a response for them close to their elaboration in cases where interviewees or people surveyed gave no specific written response. In most cases, the answers for the system-wide perspective (such as in Canada or Switzerland) were very straightforward: they were more decentralized at the federal level than at the state, province, local or district level. Invariably, the answer was one or two points above the mark for the fragmentized unit. I therefore decided to generalize the answer to the rest of the observations with a two point mark-up to allow for recognition of the difference of centralization of decision-making when talking from the perspective of a country in relation to its districts or regions. This was done in cases where people did not specifically respond with two answers.

In all cases, even in countries with a very small national or federal intervention in education policy, such as Australia, the US, Canada and Switzerland, special care was taken in construing the respondents' answers. In extreme cases, like Switzerland or Canada, countries have managed to collaborate by means of inter-cantonal or inter-provincial committees or commissions aimed at designing and formulating commonly agreed policies. The US, a decentralized system with a federal education authority (the US Department of Education) is even more difficult to map. Some of the respondents complained about recent federal intervention, through the NCLB Act, in the constitutional rights of education policies of states.

The Language of Teachers and Principals

Yet another obstacle was the fact that the language of teachers, principals and experts is not the same across systems and cultures or even within the same system and culture. Teachers and principals are so focused on the processes and intricacies of teaching and learning that they sometimes disregard concepts such as vouchers, free choice, devolution of decision-power, decentralization, etc. It was very difficult for me to interview some of the teachers or principals with the same set of questions. The meaning of these words and concepts was totally alien to some, and to all generally irrelevant to their daily work. Experts from governments and academia were more amenable to these concepts and conversely, more reluctant to give definite answers. This is why answers on the issue of decentralization clustered around 4 – the neutral answer – right in the center between centralization and decentralization. Moreover, it may also be that the concept of decentralization is too broad to be unambiguously defined and so the 'lost in translation' effect often came into play and frequently I had to illustrate the meaning of decentralization by giving an example or telling a story.

In most schools, when asked, "Have you heard of PISA?" many of the principals and teachers seemed unaware of its existence – a few teachers even told me, "Oh yes, the Leaning Tower of Pisa, in Italy." Teachers and principals from all over my sampled world were more concerned about the processes and their views within their own school than with issues of best or good practices and policies, though in countries such as Finland, England, Scotland and New Zealand, the people that I talked to knew about PISA.

Reducing Qualitative Answers into Numbers

In the end I saw my task as a translator of concepts, trying to convey the same idea to all respondents, to ensure that they understood the ideas and real meaning behind all questions and that I understood the real meaning of their answers. I tried to collect this information by ranking the responses on a scale of 1 to 7. For the centralization–decentralization continuum, a response of 1 in my survey meant a very centralized system in almost all aspects while 7 meant a much more decentralized system in policies and practices, with no single central authority controlling the system or the policies of the observed entities. A response of 1, 2 or 3 would reflect the perception of a centralized system, with no devolution of power, and controlled in one way or another (where 1 is a very centralized and 3 is a loosely centralized system). A response of 5, 6 or 7 would mean a perception of a decentralized system with some devolution of power (5) or considerable devolution of power (7) to districts, school boards or authorities. A rating of 4 is the perfect undecided ambiguous answer, provided by the respondents themselves or marked by me during the interview when even after some dialogue the interviewee and I were unable to identify the perceived reality of the situation.

Figure 0.1 shows the spectrum of centralization of decision-making. These are the responses arranged by ascending median value and subsequent ordering criteria.

Figure 0.1: How centralized is the education policy in your country?

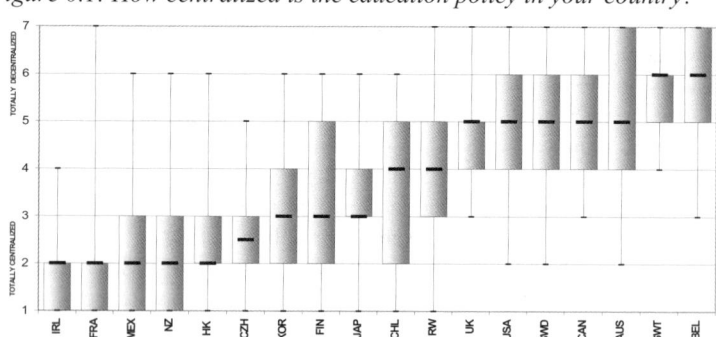

As can be seen in Figure 0.1, there is no clear pattern related to decentralization or devolution of decision-making, even though the decentralization-autonomy of schools was the policy of choice in international organizations such as the World Bank. Additionally, this was considered by many as the right thing to do in school education policy management during the 1980s and 1990s, as is documented later.

The graph shows considerable variation, from the country with the most centralized system, Ireland, as the observation furthest to the left, and the most decentralized system, Belgium (Flanders), as the observation furthest to the right of the spectrum. The median value for all high-performing countries (RW – rest of the world except Mexico and Chile) is 4. This apparent convergence to 4 does not mean that there is a pattern or similarity. On the contrary, in this analysis a 4 means that education systems and policies, as perceived by many knowledgeable people, are seen as comprising features of both centralization and decentralization of decision-making.

There is no clearly identifiable single tendency. Policies and systems world-wide, at least from the perceptions of knowledgeable people, look different. This data seems to convey that there is no convergence among high-performing countries about the issue of centralization or decentralization. School education mechanisms around the world seem to have their own *ad hoc* arrangements for managing education policies and systems. A tentative conclusion would be that countries to the left of the RW (rest of the world) observation are more centralized and countries to the right are more decentralized. However, such a generalization might encounter difficulties since the RW observation sits at a value of 4, which is not really significantly different from any of the observations in our sample, given the spread of answers in each country or system, to the spread of answers in the RW cluster, as shown by the shaded bars.

One might question this line of analysis and argue that the country-wide unit of analysis of the decentralization factor is not appropriate. This is because there are many highly centralized systems with policies in relation to schools, but highly decentralized from the territorial fragmentation of the country. This is the case for education realities in the US, Canada, Belgium, Great Britain and Switzerland. Given the limitations of my research in those countries, I tried to overcome this plausible observation by comparing, say, the US with France with such a macro-level question in two ways:

- I asked the interviewees to make a judgment about the degree of decentralization in their system, on a country-wide basis and then compare it with the degree of decentralization of their system on a regional basis. In this case the interviewees should base their comparison and evaluation on their own region, locality or state.

- The second method was to look at the question of school autonomy rather than the centralization or decentralization of decision-making. Decentralization and autonomy as policies and practices may converge in some countries but diverge in others, as the data from the survey shows or as the case-specific analysis of Mexico, New Zealand, the US and Singapore revealed (see Chapter 2).

The regional level of analysis to report on the approach to solving the question of the proper level of analysis is shown in Figure 0.2:

Figure 0.2: How centralized is the education policy in your region?

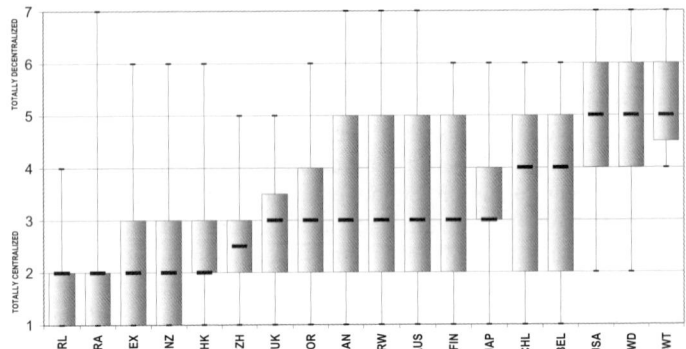

Comparing the two graphs (Figures 0.1 and 0.2) the first obvious difference is the median value for the RW observation. Figure 0.2 shows a median value of 3 rather than 4. The level of analysis is region or district-specific rather than the country-wide analysis of Figure 0.1. The number of respondents in Figure 0.2 is 451 without Mexico and Chile, and 542 with Mexico and Chile. This is probably a more accurate way of comparing education systems, looking at the level of the authority that calls the shots.

After two decades of talking and pushing decentralization, the education systems at the district or regional level of inquiry seem more centralized than decentralized. In centralized national systems that are not fragmentized (Finland, Ireland, France, Korea, Mexico and Japan) the answer is the same since they are not really divided into regions as the fragmentized systems are (the UK, the US, Canada and Switzerland).

This is why most of the countries appear to the left of the RW value with the same level of centralization and answers. There is no need to divide up the analysis of those countries with centralized national systems of education since they will show the same results. The analysis was done for all the countries or regions, to account for and compare systems that are truly fragmentized or federalized, namely those to the right of the RW observation. Figures 0.1 and 0.2 look similar, though with a slight downward shift beginning with the RW observation and countries to the right. Therefore, once interviewees were controlled by the level of observation or analysis (when asked to consider region rather than country), they downgraded their answers to show a system with more centralization of decision-making.

Methodology

Interviews and visits
Data was collected from school principals, school teachers, academics and government officials. The gathering of data was based on perception surveys or questionnaires and interviews, with the interviews with principals and education experts being in most cases in-depth. Perception-based data was collected on several topics related to education and school policies and practices. The analysis of two data sets was done on a national and a regional level. For each variable the participating countries or regions were then listed in ascending fashion from the 1 to 7 answer range.

Many of the in-depth interviews were conducted with the principals of 165 schools. Interviews with schools and experts in Chile and Mexico are not included among the high-performing countries. So, excluding Chile and Mexico, I visited 137 schools from high-performing countries. Although I made an effort to visit high-performing schools in Chile and Mexico as well, they were not included in the median or mean values of high-performing countries represented in the RW observation. When principals were not available, the interviews were conducted with deputy or assistant principals, although this was the exception. These in-depth interviews were complemented by question-naires given to teachers, often completed together with a short interview. Some of the questionnaires were completed by teachers without an interview for two reasons: a) Teachers were not available at the time of my visit; b) Principals asked me to send or leave the questionnaires without granting an interview. In all cases, principals were asked to convey to teachers the meanings of questions in case of doubts. Fewer than five teachers referred queries to me by e-mail. Unfortunately, I did not keep a record of the teachers who were eventually interviewed as usually at the beginning all the teachers were present. In my estimate, 70 per cent of teachers were interviewed.

In all countries, in-depth interviews were also carried out with experts (governmental and academic) in education policies, using similar questionnaires. Some academics were not available at the time of my visit and the interview was conducted by phone. In some cases I received an e-mail reply to the questionnaire. The goal was to interview at least one expert from each country. In most cases more than two experts per country were interviewed. In total, 59 academic and 56 government experts were interviewed in all countries.

A third group of experts, international experts, was chosen to answer similar questions, but framed in a more global or ideal model of education policy. Instead of asking the international experts: "How autonomous are public or private schools, like your school, in your country when making decisions?" I would frame the idea as follows: "Autonomy in schools is key to education quality (such as performance in international [national] evaluations [assessments])". The idea was to create a benchmark of experts' perceptions, most of them related to or familiar with the work of PISA, to facilitate analysis of comparisons among countries or regions. Six of the 15 experts interviewed are, or were at the time of the interviews, PISA-related OECD expert staff; two were UNESCO experts in education; four of them were related to PISA either as country contacts or national project managers, or as technical members or consultants from international agencies working for PISA; two were experts from the European Union in areas of school policies and one was a university professor who has taken part in international studies of various sorts in secondary education.

Although the main tool of data gathering was the interview, I decided to design a questionnaire to help me to condense the data for further analysis and interpretation. This also helped me to conduct all the interviews and all the visits in a consistent, homogenous way. The same questionnaire was applied to all different nations or regions. The survey or questionnaire contained a core section identical in all surveys for all interviewees. Variations of the questionnaire were then designed for the different clusters of interviewees, namely principals, teachers, government experts, academic experts and international experts. At the request of some prospective interviewees, the questionnaires were available in five different languages: Spanish, English, French, Korean and Japanese. Translations into French, Korean and Japanese were made with a back-and-forth interaction between the translators and me in search of meaning of words and significance. Nevertheless, when there were any doubts or questions during the interviews, I could clarify them at once. In France, Korea, and Japan, I conducted the interviews with the help of a translator or student (fluent in English, Spanish and the language of concern). As it turned out, even though French authorities requested a translation and an interpreter, all principals and most teachers were able to handle the interviews in English or Spanish. Most of the questions in the questionnaire were given a 1 to 7 ordinal scale. Figure 0.3 shows an example:

Figure 0.3: Example of the scale of 1 to 7 type question

How autonomous are public schools in your country at the lower secondary level (or upper secondary level) when making decisions?

a. Overall

Zero autonomy	1	2	3	4	5	6	7	Total autonomy

b. School curriculum

Zero autonomy	1	2	3	4	5	6	7	Total autonomy

The use of parenthesis in the question means that interviewees were asked to answer each question from the perspective of their own school, lower secondary or upper secondary since the target student population were 15-year-old pupils. Some of the questions had a multiple-choice answer. The following is an example of a multiple-choice question:

Figure 0.4: Example of the multiple-choice questions

How is the class selection (students in class [or grouping]) decided in your school?

School	
a.	At random
b.	By GPA[7]
c.	By gender balance
d.	By cultural diversity
e.	By alphabetic order
f.	By IQ
g.	By behavioral attitude
h.	By parents' request
i.	Other

[7]GPA: Grade point average

A confidential profile section was included in the questionnaire to allow me to identify the school visited and interviewees interviewed from the list of schools and expert ranks. A list of the final questions (to principals, the longest questionnaire) is available on request. School interviews were complemented by a short visit to the premises of all schools, and where possible, a short observation of mainly mathematics and English classes. The visit to a school lasted about three hours on average. The typical protocol was:

- Arrival, usually early or mid-morning
- Interview with the principal (from forty-five minutes to one-and-a-half hours, depending on the time allotted by principals to the interview)
- Interview with teachers separately or together, depending on the time available to teachers (interviews lasted from twenty to forty-five minutes)
- Tour of the school premises[8]

Often I was invited to stay for lunch either at facilities shared by students and teachers or in special dining facilities reserved for teachers and staff only. In most cases I was allowed to take photographs, although in many schools I was requested not to photograph students' faces.

The sample of schools was based on careful consideration rather than on a random criterion with the help of an informed party in each of the visited countries or regions. In some countries there are no lists of high-performing schools available. In other countries, this type of information is not available to the public. When available, the information was either not comparable or the validity of the information was questionable since in many cases the information was not official. The only way to obtain a list of high-performing schools was through an

---

[8] School premises included principals' offices; administrative offices; teachers' social lounge; teachers' work or office lounge; students' lounge (many schools have students' lounges ranging from very large agora-type halls to very small rooms); typical classrooms; mathematics and science classrooms; science laboratories; workshops (usually for metal and woodwork); computer and information technology rooms; painting and sculpture classrooms; home-economics classrooms; design and textile laboratories; music classrooms and studios; sports facilities; social events facilities, and from time to time special areas unique to some schools such as school museum, chapel, meditation and prayer rooms, students' and staff nursery, parents' lounge, secluded gardens and special education sections and facilities.

informed party, usually a professor or a public official working in an agency related to education policy. Sometimes, when they were willing and available, the Mexican Embassy acted as an intermediary to facilitate access to the best available information from a better-informed party. However, in most cases I had to find my own way to access such a person. I am confident that the schools selected are indeed high-performing schools in each country or region – from the point of view of schools where students obtained high marks in standardized exams, or schools that added high value, or schools that enjoyed a high reputation in the opinion of the better-informed party or parties.

Access to schools and experts
The next hurdle that needed to be overcome was gaining access to schools. Not all schools were available; nor were all schools open to the research. However, most of the sampled schools were sympathetic to the project and kindly and eagerly opened their doors. It was not possible to obtain a similar number of schools in each country or region. Nor was it possible to gain similar or symmetrical distributions of schools by size, ownership or management (namely public, private subsidized and private independent). However, even with all the resources and all the support available, it would not have been possible to make up enough sizeable, homogenous samples of different kinds of schools.

In most cases, the questionnaires were sent in advance (one or two weeks before the actual visit). In many cases the surveys were requested in advance so as to secure access to the schools. The survey was sent ahead in order to save time for principals and teachers during the interview and visit to schools. Experts were sent the questionnaires in advance in most cases. Very few people (only two schools and three participants as I recall) declined the interview after reviewing the questionnaires.

Non-random sample
Non-random-based studies of international policies and practices using different levels of analysis have been conducted before. There are groups of people who try to find other types of patterns, convergences or universals with similar methodologies, namely non-random samples based on structured visits, observations and interviews across different countries. However, these have been at the level of analysis of the classroom or the subjects, such as mathematics. In this line of research we find the work of two projects: International System for Teacher

Observation and Feedback (ISTOF, preceded by ISERP)[9] and The International Center for Classroom Research (ICCR)[10]

In each case teams of experts from different countries conducted their work based on *in situ* observations, interviews, videos, and analysis of school policies and school and classroom practices as they relate to teaching and learning. They are similar to my project in the non-random methods of selecting schools and in the search of patterns, but they are different in the level of analysis and methodology of collecting data (many researchers as opposed to one researcher).

Management, Reduction of Data and Graphs

The interviews were not videotaped or recorded. The only written sources of data are therefore the completed questionnaires and my research notes. The questionnaires were very detailed and had answers on a scale of 1 to 7. This was done primarily in order to save time for interviewees and help my recollection of answers. However, the 1 to 7 rating scale for most questions was chosen as a means of reducing qualitative perception answers to an ordinal arrangement of preferences. In this way content analysis was not needed because with this method the content analysis was done as close as possible to the source of the information, namely the interviewee and the questionnaire.

All questionnaires were answered directly by interviewees or by me in front of the interviewees. The questionnaires were then transferred to data sets in a spreadsheet format. The spreadsheet was arranged in such as way as to facilitate manipulation by a specialized statistics software package. Exploratory analysis of the data was done for the first quartile, median, third quartile, maximum, minimum, mode, mean and standard deviation values for each question. The graphs were drawn with the help of spreadsheet-type software. Data for the graphs was arranged in such a way as to obtain a stepped pattern. In order to arrange the graphs in this pattern, each observation was ordered by the following criteria in ascending order: 1) Median value; 2) first quartile; 3) third quartile; 4) mean value; 5) standard deviation

How to Read the Graphs

Graphs are to be read from left to right in ascending order. The vertical axis shows the ascending order of answers (variables) from all interviewees to the 1 to 7 format questions. The horizontal axis shows

---

[9] See more about ISTOF and ISERP in Chapter 1 footnotes 9 and 10.

[10] Information about ICCR may be found at http://www.edfac.unimelb.edu.au/ ict/iccr/ and http://extranet.edfac.unimelb.edu.au/DSME/lps/.

the countries or regions of the world (categories) in ascending order according to criteria listed above.

For example, Figure 0.5 shows a median value of 4 for the RW observation. This is a neutral value. It means that countries are not following a recipe for autonomy of schools (see Chapter 4). Each bar in the graph depicts an observation for a given country or region; say, IRE for Ireland or MEX for Mexico or CHL for Chile.

Figure 0.5: How autonomous are schools in your country at the compulsory level when making decisions?

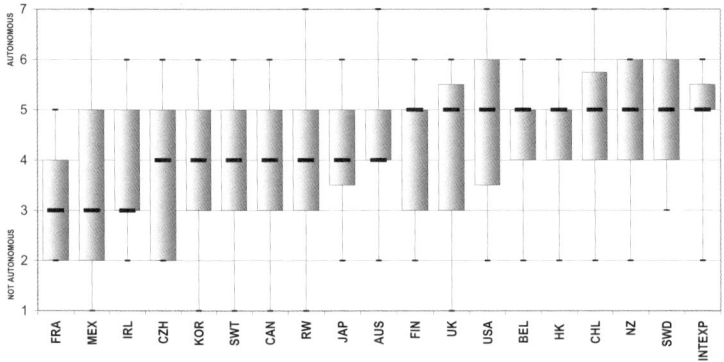

One of the ways of construing the variation of answers in each country, region or observation, as depicted by the gray bars in each graph and the maximum–minimum value depicted by thin lines in each observation, is to look at two possible explanations:

- That school systems and policies are in a state of flux.
- That it is difficult to understand concepts such as decentralization (or autonomy) with a single meaning for all people, even within the same region or school.

In any event, as shown in the graph, all answers show a pattern. The median answer from the international experts given here as a benchmark means that they believe that more autonomy is better than less. However, the international experts do not appear to want to see schools totally autonomous, since the median answer 5 is not far from the median answer 4 for the RW.

The Organization and Contents of the Monograph
The data findings reported in this monograph were obtained from 565

perception questionnaires completed by 165 school principals, 270 teachers, 59 academics, 56 government officials and 15 international experts from 19 countries around the world. Chapter 1 sets out the theoretical background to the research. The study falls within the purview of the field of international education and it draws specific lessons for low-performing countries. Moreover, connections between external and domestic forces were analyzed, highlighting the roles of international organizations. The study was conducted against the background of the comparative education approach of borrowing and lending policies and practices. Theorists in this field lay the foundations for understanding the conditions for transfer and the hurdles to borrowing and lending. Some attempt at framing the research is made in explaining the findings according to the propositions of sociologists in Actor Network Theory in analyzing power relations and how things really happen in group interactions (Callon 1986; Latour 1986, 2005).

Chapter 2 narrows the analysis to decentralization and autonomy as the main topics of analysis. After a general overview, the literature is narrowed even more to the decentralization or devolution of decision-making in Mexico. In line with many theorists and empiricists, I conclude that the devolution of power and autonomy mean different things to different people and that movements to transfer, lend or borrow these ideas or policies arrive in significantly different ways when exported from one culture or system to the next. These findings seem to contradict a vision of convergence in school education and a vision of best practices and benchmarks.

The comparison between the two visions and the role of international organizations is discussed further in Chapter 3, where the convergence theories (Boli et al 1985; McNeely & Cha 1994; McNeely 1995; Kamens et al 1996; Meyer et al 1997; Baker & LeTendre 2005) and benchmark proponents (World Bank 1995, 1999a, 1999b, 2004b; OECD 2001, 2004, 2005a, 2005b, 2006) are contrasted with the suggestions of Dale (2001, 2005, 2006), Crossley (1999, 2000), Crossley & Jarvis (2001), Crossley & Watson (2003), O'Neill (1995), Popkewitz (1996), Schriewer (1992), Schriewer & Martínez (2004), Steiner-Khamsi (2003, 2004) and Steiner-Khamsi & Stolpe (2004). This chapter also draws on the evidence and findings from the research field, covering decentralization and autonomy. It reviews the literature on the same topic by the OECD and compares the OECD's findings with those of this research. Findings may guide policy-makers and international organizations as to the lending power limits of international studies.

Chapter 4 reviews the convergence or divergence discussion in issues such as curricula, timetables, hiring and firing of teachers, evaluation, assessments and accountability. As in Chapter 3, evidence seems to suggest that international organizations should use even more reflexive language since many factors, including culture, institutions, national and local politics, translations and situations or contexts, limit transferability or ubiquity of policies, processes and practices.

In the final chapter conclusions are drawn and suggestions are made. There seems to be little argument that policy-makers at the national level face tough decisions – should they centralize policies by suggesting to local authorities what to do? Or, should they retreat to a more 'rules of the game' framework, based on targets or standards (Ravitch 1995), stimuli and accountability? It is difficult to reach definitive conclusions from perception-based analysis as in the end we are only given some indication of what people think. However, comparative quantitative studies of factors that appear to be related to high performance in school education gain much from perceptions' analysis and narrative stories. Perceptions and narratives tell a lot about the conditions, history, situations, and political and group power interactions behind schools and league tables. Every school has its own story to tell.

1

A Global Model of Education?

Comparative Education and Traveling Policies

Entering the field of comparative education is like facing an identity crisis – or so say some scholars in the field (see for example, Schriewer 1992; Broadfoot 2003b). Others note that comparative education offers a method of accumulating knowledge about an equally complex field and discipline, education or "educology" (Olivera 1992). But comparative education is complicated by the many sub-fields or related fields of inquiry that make it difficult for any single researcher to define. Different approaches, theories and methods complicate the issue even further (Epstein 1992). When doing new research in comparative education in general, one faces the problem of knowing which road to follow.

The researcher has to deal with terms such as 'globalization', 'internationalization', 'mundialization', 'supranationalization', 'school choice', 'parental choice', 'marketization', 'standardization', 'accountability' and 'assessment' of all sorts and depths. These are in addition to the established social, economic and cultural structures in the sociology of education; costs, benefits, efficiency and incentives in the economics of education; institutions and policy changes in the history of education and education and law; and school effectiveness, school improvement, school change and school reform. A newer set of concepts and propositions has emerged with terms such as leadership, learning cycles, learning teams, 'neo-comparative learnology' (Broadfoot 1999), 'learning and knowledge' (Hargreaves 2003), 'post-comparative education' and 'post-modernism' (Broadfoot 1999). Though many of these approaches are appealing and apply to the understanding and framing of my own research, questions about the eclectic nature of the field (Ninnes & Gregory 2003, p.279) and the erratic makeup of my agenda that denoted a certain fluidity in my study (Cowen 2003, p.299), raised issues about the veracity of my focus. Moreover, it also seemed to me that there appeared to be no clear sense of direction to be garnered from the field; on the contrary, the field of comparative education appeared to be "promiscuous [and] seduced, it seems, by every passing dandy" (Broadfoot 2003b, p.275).

The field of comparative education is in constant change. New ideas, new propositions, theories and emphases arise as more influential works are published. The difficulties in this field stem from both its

24

comparative component and its educational component. Dale (2005) summarizes the difficulties facing the field and warns comparative educationalists about future research endeavors. A "methodological nationalism" (p.124), "embedded statism" (p.128), and the more eclectic view of governance challenge the comparative analysis of social sciences. Here decision-making is divided among different players including the state. There is lack of evidence "of convergence between nation-states in their decisions and responses to the common challenges that they face" (p.130). Then there is the "floatingness of education" that carries many "different meanings and connotations" (p.134).

Different groups of experts claim that the field has had a significant re-emergence. Other groups of experts claim that there is really nothing or very little to compare – nothing that can be transferred from one system to the next. In the education and comparative education fields this claim is supported by the work of Coulby, Cowen & Jones (2000), Lindblad and Popkewitz (2004a, 2004b), Steiner-Khamsi (2003, 2004), Steiner-Khamsi & Stolpe (2004), Schriewer (1992), Zymek & Zymek (2004), among others. In the wider field of sociology, sociobiology, socio-technology, science and organizations, Latour, Law, Callon, and Czarniawska[1] make similar claims. I attempted to draw lessons from these relatively new approaches because I believe that they shed some light on the understanding of my research.

Comparing systems, regimes and policies does not make one a researcher of comparative and international education. Nonetheless, the first stepping-stones of comparative education were based on travelers' tales (Crossley & Watson 2003 p.12) of education systems or students' performance. Over time researchers in the field of comparative and international education have developed complex generalizations that have helped those in search of 'traveling lessons.' There are theories, methods and methodologies that frame the analysis and help the researcher to focus their research findings. However, when facing basic research questions the researcher has to decide—among other things—

---

[1] The works of Callon 1986, Latour 1986, 1988 and Law 1986a, 1986b are often cited (Latour 2005, p.10) as the initiators of a field of study known as Actor Network Theory (ANT) and Serres as the initiator of the translation approach in the social sciences (Czarniawska & Sevón 2005, p.8). Very little has evolved from these new approaches into the field of education and even less into school education. The comparative education field is ripe for such cross-fertilization. There are two chapters – one by Hedmo et al. (2005) and one by Olds (2005) – of this type of approach in *Global Ideas* by Czarniawska and Sevón (2005). Although these chapters refer to higher education, they give an insight into comparative and traveling stories and ideas in a narrative way.

whether to remain at the national level or dig into a comparative or international perspective of education systems and policies. Given the broad focus of my research and, following the advice of Mortimore (1998, pp.147, 169), to quote Robert Frost, I chose "the road less traveled."

Accumulating knowledge in the field of comparative education has been difficult for the discipline. The identity crisis in defining the field of study reflects this difficulty. In my construction, in a modern sense, knowledge that does not accumulate is not knowledge. As put forward by Crossley (1999, p.249): "At the heart of this highly charged debate are calls for educational research to be more cumulative...". This is probably the main criticism of research in education (Crossley 1999, p.249), comparative education and international education as fields or disciplines of research (Crossley & Watson 2003 pp.18-19). In order to address this criticism and following the advice of Val D. Rust (2000), associate editor of *Comparative Education Review* (CER), I resolved to tell my readers where my findings and research were coming from, though as Czarniawska (1998, pp. vi, 19) reminds us, "there is no method, strictly speaking, in social sciences." Thus, it is not surprising that finding my way through the jungle was tough.

Immersed in the field of comparative education, I was attempting to understand the shape and nature of the stones from other hills (Broadfoot 1999). This is what comparative educationalists do. Eventually, this would assist me to understand my own 'hill' – the challenges of the Mexican education system and its policies – and perhaps be able to improve them using the polished jades of others (Broadfoot 1999). After three years of research, I came to agree with Broadfoot and Watson (cited by Broadfoot 1999, p.218) that, in the analysis of all education policy and systems from a comparative perspective, culture, history and context need to be internalized (see among others, Crossley 1999, 2000, Crossley & Jarvis 2001, Crossley & Watson 2003, Bjork 2003 and Phillips 2004, p.55). Failure to consider local, contextual and historical traditions may give an inadequate picture of reality. When applied to education policy, the result may be failure. However, the discovery of these propositions on the importance of history, culture, situation or context seemed obvious and naive. I was more interested in knowing the intricacies of policies and practices, and when or if they would translate, than in discovering the seemingly obvious proposition that culture matters.

World Culture or Convergence View
There are those who support a less complex and more linear view of education. They are located on the more stable and yet 'shallower'

waters of convergence (Hartley 2003). In issues of governance or new public management in education and some other issues and trends as influenced by international organizations (McNeely & Cha 1994), there is a group of international and comparative educationalists who conclude that education policies or education features are converging (Boli et al 1985; McNeely 1995; McNeely & Cha 1994; Kamens et al 1996; Meyer et al 1997; Baker & LeTendre 2005; Stromquist 2002). These are theorists who claim that the new forces (powers) of globalization, internationalization and transnationalization have shaped or are shaping significantly similar responses in education systems and education policies around the world.

International organizations such as the World Bank and the OECD, although with different views (Robertson 2005, p.151), have their own conclusions about how children ought to be educated in this globalized, competitive and knowledge-based world economy. They have their views on how to shape systems and policies, and how politicians and policy-makers should react and steer change (OECD 2004a, pp.265-268; OECD 2005b). Nonetheless, their views of convergence, shared by many others, such as Brown and Lauder (1996, p.12), are challenged by those who see the world of education policies across boundaries as eclectic or an outcome of centrifugal–centripetal forces or tendencies (Broadfoot 2003a, p.3). The external forces are there, but the national responses have resisted convergence (Dale & Robertson 2002). Dale concludes that "there is little sign of convergence between nation-states in their decisions and responses to the common challenges they face" (2005, p.130).

International Education
This project was originally undertaken with the purpose of understanding international education (Crossley & Watson 2003) since my research looked not only at the comparability of policies and ideas from one system to the next, but also at the transferability of those policies and ideas for improvement and development. If a convergence of education policies and practices with the same meaning could be found, then the transference of policies could be a viable option in the area of international education. Should the trends be so widespread and common in high-performing countries, then top-down (supply-driven) recommendations or policy loans tied to formulas could be seriously encouraged. These would include those from organizations such as the World Bank (Torres, R. 2003, p.377, in the case of Latin America and Imam 2005, p.482, for Bangladesh, Stromquist 2005, p.103, in general) to 'help' developing or emerging countries in their challenge of educa-

tional development.

However, if convergence is not assured – and should context, history and political interactions, national, local and group politics prevent such recipes from transferring to other contexts or cultures – then the prospects of a quality of education for all as 'dictated' by international organizations with top-down policy formulas is open to question.

Units of Analysis: Global and Local

This complexity of comparative education stems also from the variety of units of analysis (Broadfoot 1999, pp.223-224) and the changing and asymmetrical nature of the units being compared or observed. It can only be explained by the context, history, culture and the human and political interactions of each education system, as was so eloquently pointed out by the oft-quoted Sadler more than a hundred years ago:

> A national system of Education is a *living thing*, the outcome of forgotten struggles and difficulties, and of 'battles long ago.' It has in it some of the secret workings of national life (1900, p.310). [My italics]

One of Sadler's main lessons:

> We cannot wander at pleasure among the educational systems of the world, like a child strolling through a garden, and pick a flower from one bush and some leaves from another, and then expect that if we stick what we have gathered into the soil at home, we shall have a living plant (Sadler 1900, p.310; cited too by Crossley 1999, p.250; Phillips 1989, p.269).

If we are to compare, we need to be aware of many factors. In each system there are contextual, historical, political and cultural underpinnings that are hurdles to translation and implementation. Phenomena described in the same way may have a completely different meaning when transposed from one context or system to another. This is perhaps the most enlightening discovery of my research and travels. We need to be aware of the difficulties of making generalizations, and at least convey the idea that the story behind comparisons is more complex than mere comparison of league tables suggests.

The world we live in is globalized, highly interconnected, and in many instances highly interdependent. Not only is there an increased need for knowledge of how other people do things, but also an increased use of statistical data. The growing interest in standardization of data among international organizations such as the OECD, the World Bank and UNESCO, and the pressure from the first two to extend their agenda, has triggered a change in organizational and research focus in agencies such as UNESCO. One is left with mixed views. Locality and globality are both important factors in explaining change. It is difficult to decide which aspect has more impact. While most analysts recognize the influence of both they usually come out in support of either local or global factors.

Can All Schools Succeed in a Global World?

We want all schools to succeed. But can they all succeed in a global and globalizing world? We want schools to succeed so that the students are champions in whatever contests or comparisons they face. Contests of life and contests of learning – quality education with high ethical, academic, civic and compassionate standards is a most desirable goal.[2] In a global and globalizing world there is the perception that many areas—school education for instance—have to change or are already changing to receive and respond to the forces of globalization and interconnectedness (Stromquist 2002a).

Whether one looks at the responses from a neo-Fordist approach (marketization) or post-Fordist approach (interventionism), education policy everywhere is affected (Brown & Lauder 1996). Regardless of the market or government response, the globalization of markets means that children will be subjected to fierce competition in schools. The increasing demand for league table studies is evidence that policy makers see school education through the lens of competition. After all, school education, job markets and global economies are connected (Rubner 2006, p.270). It is ironic that some countries are trying to move away from this type of school competition, but the global and com petitive economies, the new ways of capitalism, drag them back to the competitive arena. This type of competition in education has been so fierce that it is even considered a disease. In Korea, for example, we saw *gukyukbyeong* or 'sixth grade disease,' with students competing for places in primary schools, and *jungsambyeong* or 'ninth grade disease' for places in lower secondary school (Lee 2005).

One could argue that in a globalized economy success is measured not only in terms of goods and markets, but also in terms of education of children. Sooner or later students will attempt to enter the work force.

---

[2] The issue of quality education is not, as Mortimore (1998, p.148) points out, an issue without debate. Therefore, I have qualified education in a very broad sense to include as many aspects as possible.

If they do not enter the labor market successfully, this will be seen by some as a measure of both economic and educational failure. Education and markets have never before been so interconnected – or so it seems. Yet globalization may be changing the way education is currently seen and structured. 'Education is not enough' – the quotation attributed[3] to Henry M. Levin or derived from Levin and Kelley (1994) – raises the point that elements and 'institutions' other than school education help to explain people's access to jobs and job creation within economies.

Globalization, Performance and Measurements

In a global economy, performance is constantly measured. However, there is a case for more measurements if globalization and competitive forces shape education. As these forces have also influenced research in comparative education, the field appears to have entered the chronology of measuring the 'other':

> In a world defined through a flux of communication and interdependent networks, the growing influence of comparative studies is linked to a global climate of intense economic competition and a growing belief in the key role of education in the endowment of marginal advantage. The major focus of much of this comparative research [2000's research] is inspired by a need to create international tools and comparative indicators *to measure* the 'efficiency' and the 'quality' of education. (Novoa & Yariv-Mashal 2003, pp.424-425. Original italics; my parenthesis.)

A study of educational literature world wide reveals that there is strong evidence to state that this is an era of measurement, comparison in education (Stromquist 2002a, p.xiv) and accountability. According to Roger Dale, it all began with a document published by a truly global organization that was accountable to no one, namely the OECD. With the title, *Shaping the 21st Century: The Contribution of Development Co-operation*, this document set the stage for goals and international policies in many areas such as education.[4] Coincidentally, the education committee at the OECD was developing new ideas for education that

---

[3] Point raised by Prof. R. Dale during a personal interview in his office at the University of Bristol, on April 4, 2006.

[4] Prof. R. Dale during a personal interview in his office at the University of Bristol, on April 4, 2006.

ended up in PISA[5]. OECD (OECD 1996, p.2):

> We also recognize that those responsible for public funds are accountable for its effective use. We have a duty to state clearly the results we expect and how we think they can be achieved.

> It is time to select, taking account of the many targets discussed and agreed at international level for a limited number of indicators of success by which our efforts can be judged.

In education this has been of paramount importance and it is changing the way things should look and how policy should be shaped – at least at the perception level of policy-makers. Again the growing demand for international league tables is evidence of this. One facet of education that PISA attempts to measure is school education outcomes based on competencies rather than contents. Based on this, PISA is trying to distinguish aspects that work from aspects that do not, to be able to cope with real life difficulties or decisions in this competitive world.

If elements that matter in one policy context are found to be able to 'travel' – be borrowed from or lent to any country – then we have convergence, with policies and practices everywhere becoming more and more similar.[6] If these elements are not able to travel, then the world diverges in school education policy. Thus the two views are significantly different in their scope of explaining why things are the way they are.

Making Schools Work: Globalization, School Improvement and Effectiveness

Millions of minds around the world from very different epistemologies are working actively towards the goal of making schools work so that our children succeed. Notwithstanding this, no definite outcome has emerged as the best practice approach.

> In spite of the huge, and continuing, expenditure of resources in time, money and human endeavour, recorded in an enormous body of literature on educational change, it has not been noteworthy to date in bringing about changes of the order and scale required to have a systematic and durable impact on school systems and

---

[5] The birth of PISA as described by Andreas Schleicher in an interview in his office at the OECD headquarters on April 23, 2004.

[6] Interview with Prof. R. Dale. See footnote 4.

classroom practice. (Hall & Carter 1995, p.171)

Perhaps in this particular topic of education reform and change, or factors that really matter in determining success in the quality of education, there are 'many ways to skin a cat.'[7] Or perhaps there is not a universal global answer at all. This might be because the correct mix of policies and practices, aimed at effecting change in a positive and consistent way towards students' achievement (goals, targets, indicators of education) is context-specific – "context matters" (Crossley 1999, pp.251, 263; Crossley 2000, p.323; Crossley & Jarvis 2001; Scott 2005)[8]– history-specific and culture-specific (Grant 2000, Broadfoot 2001; Phillips & Ochs 2003, p.458). We may never get a single convergence at the policy level. The measures of educational success are flawed and, given the nature and complexities of school education, we may never find the ideal formula for measuring education.

After looking at the evidence collected through my research it is my understanding that, notwithstanding the force of globalization, education is still a local phenomenon. Although nation-states are not the only players, they are still the most important ones. National and local forces are perhaps more relevant than global or international forces:

> . . . most if not all decisions about the shape and direction of national education systems continue to be taken by the states themselves. (Dale 2005, p.130)

However, the literature on school improvement and school effectiveness has been directed specifically at searching for those global factors. At different times these factors have been identified. For example, eleven factors were described by Stoll and Mortimore (1997), ten principles of "authentic school improvement" were proposed by Hopkins (2004) and Mortimore (1998) outlined specific factors as well. School improvement has also traveled. In particular, under the auspices of ISERP[9] and ISTOF,[10] researchers of school improvement claim that

---

[7]   Dr. Mark Mason of the Comparative Education Research Centre at the University of Hong Kong raised this point in an interview on October 14, 2004.

[8]   Context matters not only for students' academic achievement but for actual segregation of students. School choice programs without due attention to context would tend to increase segregation rather than integration. This is the conclusion of Scott's work (2005, p.3) and a view shared by Levin (2005, p.viii).

[9]   ISERP: The International School Effectiveness Research Project.

[10] ISTOF (The International System for Teacher Observation and Feedback) is organized by many people in 20 countries or regions, with Prof. David

some school and classroom factors ("universal factors") travel across countries (Reynolds et al. 2002).

Globalization and International League Table Studies

Adding to this pressure for change and the complexities of explaining how things happen in the real world, there is still the work of a totally different group of experts. These are the professionals in charge of designing, implementing and construing the results of international league table studies such as PIRLS, TIMSS and PISA.

With complex statistical tools, multivariate and regression analysis, this group of international experts makes direct suggestions about policies or practices that appear to work better than others across countries (OECD 2001, 2004a, 2005b, 2006; Schleicher 2005, 2006a, 2006b). Their work is based primarily on a narrow but precise measurement of education through standardized tests and correlations based on factual and perceived data through the results of examinations and context questionnaires. This is precisely the kind of world described by the OECD's 1996 publication, *Shaping the 21st Century.*

This work attracted international attention and demand by an increasing number of governments. Year after year more countries or national systems of education swell the ranks of international assessments sponsored by the International Association for the Evaluation of Educational Achievement (IEA), UNESCO or the OECD. Governments are probably lured by the belief that, if properly applied, best policies and practices will significantly improve the performance of students. The suggestion is that such students would be better equipped to face life or further their studies in this increasingly complex and globalized world. Yet the critics in the area of sociology of education and of school improvement and school effectiveness seem to offer evidence that dwarfs the findings of these monumental efforts in the search for pattern and factors.

The efforts of international organizations seem to feed the need for change, providing an impulse for further bolstering change in the policy arena or "preconditions for borrowing" (Phillips & Ochs 2003, p.452) or stimuli for attraction (Phillips 2004, pp.54-55). Awareness about globalization or other stimuli for change has increased the impulse for

---

Reynolds, School of Education, University of Plymouth, UK, playing a key role. For an in-depth account, see Reynolds et al 2002. Information about ISTOF may be found at http://www.icsei.net/.

more comparisons, more and more pressures for policy borrowing or "cross national attraction" (Phillips 2004, p.55). Can these suggestions or policies travel across countries? Yes, and no. Countries included in my survey share some of the names or labels of policies and practices, however, when comparisons looked at the meaning of such policies and practices countries and systems of education vary a lot. However, I would argue that, although globalism and globalization have increased measurement, assessment, comparisons and the perceived utility of policy borrowing and policy lending, they have at the same time increased the need for understanding all these phenomena.

From the comparative and international education perspective, systems of education seem to work like a black box. Finland is a good example of perceptions and misperceptions as to the reasons for success.

In any case, the Finnish 'miracle of PISA' no longer appears to be a miracle. To put it simply, it is still possible to teach in the traditional way in Finland because teachers believe in their traditional role and pupils accept their traditional position. Teachers' beliefs are supported by social trust and their professional academic status, while pupils' approval is supported by the authoritarian culture and mentality of obedience. The Finnish 'secret' of top-ranking may therefore be seen as the curious contingency of traditional and post-traditional tendencies in the context of the modern welfare state and its comprehensive schooling (Simola 2005, pp.465-466).

It is tempting to think that at least some of the authority of Finnish teachers is based on their relatively strong professional identity, which enables them to season their traditional teaching with the spice of progress. It is also tempting to think that at least some of the obedience of Finnish students stems from the natural acceptance of authority, and the ethos of respect for the teacher (Simola 2005, p.466).

Globalization and Convergence
Another group of people, with its own sociology of knowledge, has suggested that very specific forces or trends are shaping the school education world. These forces include globalization, competitiveness and open markets (Ball 1998; Carnoy & Rhoten 2002; Davies & Guppy 1997; Mok & Tan 2004; Mok & Chan 2002; Mortimore 2001; Cheung & Sidhu 2003; Stromquist 2002a, 2002c). Some try to explain changes

in school education as a reaction to these trends (Mok 2004; Stromquist 2002a, p.13). Others see the phenomenon as a backward relationship, describing how education "provides individuals and communities with ways of both engaging with and navigating a way through the difficulties of globalization" (Soudien, pp.145-146; Stromquist 2002a, p.13 and Stromquist 2005). There have been attempts in the literature to explain why and how some nation-states immersed in a global economy resist pressures of globalization and competitiveness by isolating the national and cultural values from the global incursions. Asian researchers tend to convey this by trying to explain the different rationales in educational change that globalization brings about (Gopinathan 2001, p.5).

There is change everywhere in school systems, not only in words but also in practice. However, the interpretation of this change is a completely different issue. Lessons from comparing Singapore with the United States provide some insight. The governance of schools has changed in both countries and competition among schools has also increased. However, in order to compare Singapore with the United States or any other Western industrialized democracy, one needs to be much more precise about the depth and meaning of the compared changes. Some countries in the West are changing out of dissatisfaction with their own performance and their own system. Some countries in the East, such as Singapore and Hong Kong, are changing to prepare already successful schools and systems for a new era (Gopinathan 2006).

For example, in the United States good things are not happening in the classrooms. In Singapore they are. The same forces are driving change but from a different perspective and for different reasons. In the United States change is driven out of a perception that schools have failed. In Singapore, the beliefs of the 'credible' government elite drive change; they view globalization as an opportunity to steer additional change and reform. The credible government elite, rather than a sense of failure, steers markets and marketization. Things happen for a reason; different contexts induce them. In Singapore, education is viewed instrumentally: what is good for the economy is good for the state. Markets and competition are good for the economy and therefore good for the state. Qualified human capital is good for the markets and therefore good for the government. An open, more diversified, more competitive education system is good for the labor markets and for the economy. So it is not the perception of failure that drives change in Singapore, but the perception of the need for the credible government elite (based on their performance) to steer the economy even further.[11]

Globalization, Trends and Convergences

Other researchers are looking into specific trends in education, not only in practices and policies but in traits, values and ideas. These include the emphasis on mathematics in all curricula, mass schooling (massification of education), schooling as an institution, policies to support ideas such as public funding, education as a public or collective good, compulsory education for all, credentials (Baker & LeTendre 2005, pp.7-8) and education as a human right. In this view, convergence occurs regardless of the cause, context or cultural differences. While the context is relevant, global factors are more important.

> Every individual school is still influenced by local, regional, and national factors, but the basic image of a school – what it is and what it should do – is commonly defined in the same way globally. Consequently, the organization of national school systems (French, German, American, and so on) is now influenced by transnational forces that are beyond the control of national policy makers, politicians, and educators themselves yet appear to be part of their everyday world (Baker & LeTendre, pp.9-10).

By the same token, scholars claim that international organizations promote and facilitate this convergence:

> An extraordinary expansion of educational systems has taken place throughout the world over the last century. This expansion has been characterized by a remarkable degree of convergence in both educational ideology and educational structure across all types of nation-states. (McNeely & Cha 1994, p.1)

For those who see a more eclectic view, global forces compensate the local forces:

> We will see that both dominant global messages and forms of local expression are in existence. Over time, however, the tendency has been much greater in the direction of uniformity than differentiation.

---

[11] Personal interview with Prof. Saravanan Gopinathan in his office at CRPP, National Institute of Education, Nanyang Technological University, Singapore, on January 6, 2006.

(Stromquist 2002, p.13)

Complex Subject

One of the difficulties in the study of education and education policy is to keep track of everything in an orderly manner. The social sciences have struggled with this for decades. With few exceptions, the construction and accumulation of knowledge in areas such as education is painful and difficult (Crossley & Watson 2003, p.8). Perhaps, it is the lack of social method: "It is doubtful whether there is any method in social sciences studies, at least in the sense of a prescribed procedure that brings about foreseeable results" (Czarniawska 1998, p.19). That is why there is such an enormous body of literature that is not necessarily consistent. There are many different studies and approaches to the knowledge of education and education policies. There are hundreds of journals and publications around the world with thousands of articles every year on similar or related topics. The published work does not necessarily fall into easy categories or groups. There are studies in education policy that borrow theoretical or methodological frameworks of analysis from areas apparently unrelated to policy or public policy, such as Lindblad and Popkewitz (2004a, 2004b) or from psychiatry or borrowing from epidemiology research (Levin B., 1998). Studies in a well-established body and group of research such as the comparative education epistemic community through to the *Comparative Education*, *Comparative Education Review* and *Compare* journals often find themselves writing beyond the boundaries of their own field (Little 2000) or being reincarnated many times (Broadfoot 2003c).

The cross-fertilization of ideas from one group in one arena, from one system or within the boundaries of one nation or nation-state with specific expertise, has mutated like an epidemic disease. Not respecting the confines of the analysis of a given group or framework, this epidemic may bring failure when policies are imported from a different context or local context, (see for example, Hopkins 2004, p.84), or when they are implemented in day-to-day decision-making at school level or in real life.

There is enough evidence to suggest that policies fail in their goal of improving students' achievement or scores because designers bypass or underestimate the intricacies and difficulties of policies during the implementation stage (Dyer 1999). Implementation has to be planned with the same care as designing policies (O'Neill 1995; Hall & Carter 1995). Therefore studies of macro-politics and macro-policies ingrained within the boundaries of school effectiveness and school improvement that were not meant for the level of analysis of schools and therefore for the 'real or authentic' approach to school improvement (Hopkins 2004) are often found.

Macro-policies or systemic policies that do not take into account the factors directly related to schools, teachers and students will not succeed. "Unless central reforms address the context of teaching and learning, as well as capacity-building at the school level, within the context of external support, then . . . the aspirations of reform will never be realized." (Hopkins 2004, p.86) Crossley and Watson (2003) proposed a valid notion in calling for more communication between professional cultures of research, policy and action as professional cultures at the research level need to cross-fertilize more, but they also need to be closer to the professional cultures (epistemic groups) of policy-makers and practitioners.

Success
A seminal report propelled modern debate about this subject – this is The Coleman Report, a single publication that has triggered forty years of research worldwide, [12] and the debate is still continuing. Matters became even more complex with the publication of the research of Christopher Jencks et al (cited by Mortimore 1998, p.3) and Gorard (2001, p.285). In summary, the authors of both works suggest that schools don't matter much. A single provocative proposition has generated an incalculable number of research papers, books, reviews and articles that have been published worldwide and resulting in the birth of new schools of thought and patterns of research.

The work of PISA 2000, 2003 and 2006 (at the time of writing yet to be analyzed and published) complete the forty-year leap or loop from 1966 to 2006. The findings of PISA 2003 confirm the Coleman findings and Sadler's suggestions.

The 1966 findings of the Coleman Report are remarkably consistent with the 2003 findings of the PISA/OECD Report. This is irrespective of their nature, national versus international context of the studies, and the forty years that elapsed between the two studies, the agencies or organizations or people involved in their design and implementation. Numerous other studies conducted at national levels have found much the same correlation.

The two large studies and many others (for example, Gorard 2001,

---

[12] As pointed out by Prof. David Hogan, Acting Dean, Centre for Research in Pedagogy and Practice (CRPP), National Institute of Education, Nanyang Technological University, Singapore. Personal interview in his office at CRPP, January 13, 2006.

pp.285-287, and Heckman & Masterov 2007, pp.2-3) have documented the phenomenon. The socio-economic and cultural backgrounds and contexts of schools' intake of students and their families (Hoxby 2001), have a strong correlation with the performance or academic achievement of those schools and students.

However, the socio-economic and cultural status or backgrounds of students and their families in a given school lie beyond the realm of education policy. This applies in any educational community (policy-makers, schools and teachers). It therefore seems pertinent to ask – Why bother then? Why worry about improving schools when schools influence achievement only marginally? This has given rise to one of the most serious debates in education and school policy in the last forty years. There are those who maintain that 'school matters' and that there are good and bad schools (Gorard 2001, p.285) and those of a totally different view who maintain that 'inequalities matter' (Gorard 2001, p.287).

Before the publication of the Coleman Report, from the distant world of academia, another less empirically driven view of schools' performance in the United States had shaken the education community in the States and elsewhere. This was Milton Friedman's assertion that the failure of schools in America was the result of lack of freedom of choice and competition. He placed the onus of the low performance of school education on the schools themselves. Schools do not perform well because they do not have the incentives to do so. They are faced with a wrong and perverse set of incentives.

Schools and the education policy community had it all wrong. They were not to be blamed – try as they might they could not do anything about it even if they wanted to. On the other hand, they were to be blamed, but they did not have the mix of incentives or formula to change reality.

Convergence or Divergence

The issue is not whether the systems of school education have changed or not. It is the extent to which external or internal factors – or a combination of both – explain the changes in education. We all want answers to the question: What does it matter? Various groups of experts, using different methodological approaches, have arrived at different sets of answers that I have clustered into two identifiable schools of thought, namely convergence (the effect of international forces) and divergence (the effect of domestic or local forces and interactions).

The findings of this study suggest the lack of convergence in practices and policies insofar as there is a marked absence of pedagogical theories of teaching and learning that works consistently across systems

(Dale).[13] Nor do concepts of education policies and institutions, decentralization, marketization, autonomy mean the same across nations or regimes. Broader contexts of cultures, situations and interactions appear to matter the most in these debates.

There are persistent elements in education policy that appear to converge and then appear to diverge. Why or where does this seeming contradiction come from? The answer is multifaceted. The solution lies in resorting to the help of theoretical work combined with empirical observation, such as the insightful work by Thomas S. Popkewitz (1996). The answer also comes from a combination of methodologies and methods of analysis. One needs to look at aggregated data obtained from hard numerical series such as produced by the OECD's and IEA's comparisons of system and performance and the perceptions collected from informed people in school education. The next step is to compare this information with direct observations, interviews and the opinions of specific players everywhere – such as principals, teachers, policy experts and academics – in thoughtful and insightful narratives.

One clue may come from the meaning of certain elements in education policy. If we mean ideas and/or concepts or buzzwords, or 'slogans,'[14] then, indeed, I believe that there is a sharp convergence of agreed concepts and ideas of education. These would include child-centered education policy, teacher quality and development, flexibility of schools and teachers, responsibility (accountability), professionalism, assessment, decentralization or devolution of decision-making, autonomy, school schedules or timetabling, etc. Politicians and policy-makers across systems converge at the rhetorical level.

If the elements in education policy refer to the processes, interactions or ways in which the true cognitive values of education are made into policies or 'policized', politicized and implemented across systems, within systems and beyond boundaries, then the answer may be closer to a divergent hypothesis of the world in education policy than the convergent hypothesis. The McDonald's phenomenon has promoted the idea of cultural convergence in many areas other than fast-food services. The world of school education is not at all 'McDonaldized' in the sense that Ritzer (2004, 2006) has advanced in his idea of cultural convergence.

Schools are not McDonaldized (Dale, 1994; Watson 2004, p.169);

---

[13] Personal interview with Prof. R. Dale. See footnote 4.

[14] Prof. R. Dale refers to the same idea with the word slogans. Point raised by Prof. Dale during a personal interview in his office at Bristol University on April 7, 2006.

nor are they standardized (Hallak 2000, p.21) at the level of policies and practices – perhaps only to a very slight degree in the rhetoric or 'talk' and specific inputs, traits or signs, as will be seen later. Even in Finland, where the total variance in performance as defined by the variance between schools is the lowest in PISA 2003 (OECD 2004a, p.383), each school differs in many respects.

Of course, there are common traits, such as walled classrooms, class sessions and morning schedules – there are still many two-shift schools around the world. Even these common features cannot be generalized. Among the PISA-type[15] schools that were deemed suitable samples for my work I even found classrooms without walls in many schools. There was even one school in Mexico that had to borrow facilities from a totally different morning school meant for students of different ages and following a different curriculum. Typical accommodation, as illustrated by Robin Alexander (2000), appears to be less schematic at the secondary level. There is convergence in language and ideas and discourse; yet there is divergence in meanings.

Paradoxically, countries or systems with similar ideas or concepts, techniques or processes have different outcomes and results whilst countries or systems with different ideas or concepts, and different processes or policies have similar results or outcomes. If elements in education mean different things to different people, then the implication is that we do not have a theory to explain. We cannot answer the question: What does it really matter in education and school policy across systems?

The lack of linearity in analyzing and understanding the complex relationships between inputs, policies, processes and outcomes in education policy stems mostly from the indiscriminate mixing of the meaning of elements in education research and education policy. Once the meaning of these elements is clarified, some light is shed on the complex world of education policy, whether we are talking about analyses within or between systems. This provides us with four possible answers: 1) Convergence at the rhetorical level only; 2) convergence in some inputs and outputs; 3) divergence on the real meaning of policies, processes and practices; 4) no real solution as to what really matters and what can be applied to every case in all circumstances.

School education policies have changed (Rotberg 2044; Coulby et al 2000; Johnson et al 1998; Robertson 2006a). Most education systems

---

[15] PISA-type school: a school in an urban or rural area with students between the ages of fifteen years and three months and sixteen years and two months. In theory these schools were able to be sampled as PISA schools.

that we can account for have made radical changes in school education policies. Some changes, such as those designed and implemented in New Zealand (Boston et al 1996.; Fiske & Ladd 2000), Korea, Hong Kong, Sweden, Russia, South Africa, the United States (Popkewitz 1996), Chile (OCDE 2004a; OECD 2004b; McMeeking 2004) and Nicaragua (Gershberg 1999), have had systemic effects. Others have had a less systemic effect. Still others, like Canada or Switzerland, have undergone changes only at the provincial, cantonal or district levels.

For some countries such as Mexico, change has had more of a rhetorical significance than a real effect (Gershberg 1999; Guevara 2006; Ornelas 1998; Andere 2003, 2006; Tatto 1999). It is political rather than educational – directed primarily at reaffirming the state's control over education and education policy than at sharing and devolving power and decision-making to states, localities or schools.

In general, therefore, no one questions change in education policy. The nature of change and the reasons for change are the subject of much debate.

The Need for Classification
In analyzing the data I have ended up with numerous classifications, as well as explanations about divergence or convergence. Comparing objects or observations entails the task of classification. Classifying observable objects or phenomena is as old as scientific inquiry itself. Education systems have been compared and classified for very many years. Sadler is one of the first researchers to raise the advantages and disadvantages of comparing systems around the world. Many others have also contributed to the comparability of systems of education (Brickman 1965). Broadfoot (1999, p.220), citing Brickman and Wolhuter, synthesizes in a single paragraph the history of comparative education as it relates to classification:

> Comparative education has a long history which goes back at least as far as the ancient Greek and Roman era (Brickman 1965). Commentators have suggested that comparative education has evolved through three stages. After the prehistory of 'travellers tales' came Jullien's 1817 call for the collection of data on national education systems by an international agency (Wolhuter 1997). This is commonly regarded as the beginning of the use of the term 'comparative education' and of at least one of the field's two major genres that subsequently developed. It was the beginning of a positivist approach that emphasized the systematic gathering of empirical, statistical data to inform policy-making. [Original parenthesis]

In addition to summarizing the literature on the subject of classification of education systems, Wolhuter offers alternative ways of comparing and classifying systems and policies. He ends up classifying "national education systems based on 15 conventional statistical indicators using factor analysis and cluster analysis" (Wolhuter, 1997 p.166). These statistical indicators are drawn from hard data based on *UNESCO's Statistical Yearbook*. Others have attempted less quantitative classifications. Hopper (1968), for example, classifies education systems according to the degree of centralization and standardization of selection processes of students, early segmentation of students and the criteria used by various systems to select students.[16]

In centralization and decentralization policies researchers have attempted to rank or classify education systems, as cited by Bray (2003, p.11). For more than a decade the OECD has tried to use a fairly consistent methodological approach to classify education systems according to the degree of centralization or devolution of decision-making. The OECD classification is based in turn on the methodology of van Amelsvoort and Jaap Scheerens of the University of Twente.[17] The OECD offers an alternative classification of decentralization and school autonomy, using an alternative methodology (OECD 2005b).

Agencies or international organizations such as the IEA, the OECD, the Southern and Eastern African Consortium for Monitoring Educational Quality (SACMEQ), and UNESCO's Regional Office for Latin America and the Caribbean (OREALC) have merged the comparative and classifying exercises of education systems into policy-oriented reports. The studies related to comparative education systems, in order to shed light on policy, have become more complex and more widespread. These and other international organizations or associations have compared and classified education systems and policies by means of data accumulation over a range of high and low performers or achievers in various countries and systems.

Using massive data sets these organizations have correlated their outcomes with features of education systems. In other words, they have classified education systems not only in terms of a measure of perfor-

---

[16] An earlier more general classification of systems in search of general educational patterns is used in Thut and Adams (1964) (and cited by Hopper). Hopper used the work developed by Thut and Adams as a source of information for his classification of education systems.

[17] Researchers from the Dutch entrepreneurial research university, the University of Twente, act as the Secretariat for the Network C technical group in the OECD–INES project (International Indicators of Education Systems).

mance but under specific features or aspects of education systems such as the "locus of decision-making" (OECD 2004b, Chapter D; OECD 1998, pp.292-304) and "decentralized decision-making" (OECD 2005b, pp.63-72).

Organizations such as the OECD and UNESCO have used three main sources of data to study and compare systems: 1) hard data such as enrolment rates and levels of education; 2) test data such as the results of international standardized assessments, namely PISA and the UNESCO's (1998, 2000) Latin American Laboratory for Assessment of the Quality of Education (LLECE)[18] – under the auspices of OREALC; 3) perception-based data from context questionnaires to principals, students, teachers, experts or practitioners and so on.

Some Difficulties with PISA-type Studies

After visiting the 165 schools and looking into the whole educational framework – the age range of students, the school facilities, and the way the schooling was organized – I realized that international studies such as PISA do not answer Dale's hows, whos, whys and wherefores (2006). Like many other international studies of student performance, their samples need to be much more fragmented and much larger before they can reach definite conclusions and make general suggestions. PISA-type schools differ from each other on many issues:

- The grade level of fifteen-year-old students – the sampled grade range in PISA 2003 was from Grade 7 to Grade 12
- Affiliation – public, private-dependent or private-independent, with many variations in ownership, state financing, actual governance, and policy interactions
- Many more factors as outlined in Table 5.2

For instance, from the sample of 165 schools I noted the following variations in grades:

1. Lower secondary schools only
2. Primary and lower secondary schools under one umbrella

---

[18] LLECE stands for the Spanish name: *Laboratorio Latinoamericano de Evaluación de la Educación*. This was the first regional evaluation under the auspices of OREALC. The second evaluation under OREALC has changed its name to SERCE (*Segundo Estudio Regional Comparativo y Explicativo*) [Second Comparative and Explicative Regional Study]. (See http://llece. unesco.cl/publicaciones/16.act.)

3. Lower secondary and upper secondary schools under one umbrella
4. Upper secondary schools only
5. Primary, and lower and upper secondary schools under one umbrella
6. Lower secondary school of four years
7. Lower secondary schools of three years
8. Lower secondary (intermediate) schools of two years only
9. Upper secondary schools of two years
10. Upper secondary schools of three years
11. Upper secondary schools of four years
12. Schools with two years of primary education and four years of secondary education
13. Schools with two years of primary education and six years of secondary education
14. Upper secondary schools attached to colleges
15. Upper secondary schools for those gifted in science and technology
16. Secondary schools with variations in size, segmentation and/or specialization (vocational, technical, general)
17. Lower secondary and upper secondary schools specialized in arts, music, languages

Many have expressed concern about the range of grades in PISA-sampled students (see for example, Ross et al. 2006, pp.305-306). An additional complexity is the structure and organization of schooling as set out above. It is not sufficient simply to account for grade differences, as was done by PISA 2003, or to pay very little attention to the impact of differences in grade (OECD 2004, Table A.1, p.311). Nor is it totally appropriate to compare students from Korea and Japan, where all or most of them are in Grade 10, with students from Finland, where most of them are in Grade 9 or lower. That would be an unfair comparison – a case of missing the point and the narrative behind the facts. Not only is there a one-year difference in school experience and school exposure; the environment for students, teachers, parents, principals and authorities is totally different. Grade 10 students are upper secondary students and they differ from lower secondary students and junior school students in many matters. Their regulatory framework and regulatory bodies are different, their principals are drawn from different backgrounds and the selection process of upper secondary principals is nothing like the selection process of lower secondary or primary principals. Different criteria are used for the selection and assessment of teachers too. Curricula are also different. The degree of freedom in managing school activities, the teaching and learning functions, programs and school budgets at upper secondary schools are also totally different from those at the lower levels of education. If there is to be a theory of isomorphism in school education, one needs to combine the various school levels, school regulatory frameworks, and school organizations and associations with other potentially disturbing factors.

Schools vary in leadership styles, in open-door or closed-door policies, not only from principals and teachers to students and parents, but from schools to the community. In some cultures the status of the school principal is paramount – as in England and Korea – while in some German cantons in Switzerland schools had no principals at all. In some schools the principal's office looks as if it belongs to a cabinet minister; in other schools the principal shares an office with several other people in a tiny space. There are schools that do not have an office for the principal. There are schools where there is a strong relationship between the principal and the Board, and schools where there is no relationship at all. Some schools are run by the principal and others by a committee or a Board, the teachers, or the local authority.

To make matters even more complicated, the policy frameworks for schools change from country to country, from system to system. In some systems, there are national examinations for everyone. In others, there are no examinations at all. Even in countries with national examinations at the same level, the history may be different. Some of the sampled countries have very detailed standards in contents and goals. Others have no standards at all – or only in goals and not in contents. Countries such as New Zealand are moving away from detailed curricula, while others like Finland are moving towards more detailed curricula. In some countries there is a long history of standardization, while in others they are only beginning to apply standards.

Since studies such as PISA and TIMSS compare performance based on systems at a specific moment in time, they are comparing performance based on school backgrounds that differ completely in their histories, regulations, situations and institutions. There is no attention to the changing school stories behind the differences.

International comparisons of the type conducted by the IEA, the OECD,[19] SACMEQ and OREALC need to break up their samples more and increase the size of samples. Otherwise, they need to soften or

---

[19] PISA sampled schools as different units when the same school offered more than one program (lower secondary or upper secondary), more than one shift or more than one campus (OECD 2004, Annex A, p.328). How the PISA study considered these differences and the 17 variations listed to explain the performance of students across school varieties is not clear.

qualify their language when reaching conclusions, or making claims about the whys and wherefores. Ultimately, even with greater segmentation of schools for sampling purposes, these international studies also face the lost-in-translation factor of histories, situations and regulations – or lack of transferability. If the transferability factor is not taken into account, one ends up with a fiasco such as the science policy promoted by UNESCO (Finnemore 1993) to countries where there was no scientific community at all. One can also mention the unsuccessful implementation of the life-long learning policy so heavily promoted in the 1990s (Jakobi 2006), resulting in a policy-borrowing epidemic or 'diffusion' with many different meanings. Then there is the policy confusion and disarray that arises when concepts such as decentralization or autonomy are promoted around the world, with no real common understanding of the meaning of these words or ideas across countries.

2

Borrowing and Lending Trends:
Decentralization and Autonomy

Neither a borrower nor a lender be – Shakespeare[1]

This chapter delves into different theoretical approaches as they try to explain why, on close examination, things that look similar are often not. It raises the question of what happens when one travels around the world borrowing and lending policies. Two aspects of education systems will be analyzed: decentralization of decision making and autonomy of schools.

A Theory of Translation and Actor Network Theory (ANT)[2]

Decentralization and school autonomy concepts are not foreign to comparative, international education and globalization[3] and education literatures. They are also close to the literature of borrowing and lending. When policies are borrowed, some elements may be lost in translation, as Robert Cowen[4] pointed out to me, and as ANT proponents have suggested from a totally different epistemic group. In a 'process of metamorphosis' of pedagogic policy or action some things, such as curricula, may be translated, transposed or transformed (Alexander

---

[1] From *Hamlet* (fatherly advice from Polonius to Laertes before he sets out on his travels): 'Neither a borrower nor a lender be; for loan oft loses both itself and friend, and borrowing dulls the edge of husbandry.' Burton Raffel (ed.) (2003): *Hamlet: The Annotated Shakespeare.* New Haven: Yale University Press (p.32, Act I, Scene 3). I am aware of the use of this aphorism in two papers in the field of comparative education: Phillips (1989) as the title of his paper and Peddie (1991) as the first phrase of his paper.

[2] See Introduction. Actor Network Theory (ANT) is the sociology of associations and organizations.

[3] 'In particular, the contemporary spread of decentralization policies and reforms has been the harbinger of globalization processes, seemingly proving that, indeed, "the center cannot hold" in the face of global forces' (Astiz et al. 2002, p.66). Globalization is a concept not easily defined. Stromquist (2002b, p.iii): 'Globalization is not yet a scientific construct.' Dale and Robertson (2002, p.10): ' "Globalization" is too broad and too ambiguous a term to be used unproblematically . . .'

[4] Phone interview on April 15, 2006.

48

2000, p.516; Astiz et al 2002). In education, processes, policies and practices are subject to forces of translation. Used in the general sense, theories or generalizations of translation in education are well localized in a group of writers in comparative and international education though they are beginning to attract more attention. Examples of this are Dale's paper "from comparison to translation" (2006), Alexander's "curriculum metamorphosis" (2000) and the works of translation and implementation writers described below.

The meaning of translation in education policy and comparative education is not the same as that utilized by ANT experts (see Callon's 1986 seminal work, or Latour 1986 and 2005 for translations in organizations and associations). However, I draw from the different groups or sociologies of knowledge in the hope that some of their insights can help to formulate an approach to a theory of translation, transfer (in Crossley's words) or transformation to explain divergence and convergence or best practice of school education policies and practices.

Latour (2005, p.12) explains the ANT approach by focusing on the actions of actors and 'actants' and tracing associations ('sociology of associations' instead of 'sociology of the social') rather than already assembled and stable groups. The focus is on the 'nature of what is assembled' or the nature of the state of affairs rather than the actual assembly or state of affairs. International league table studies can enlighten us about the *state* of affairs but shed little or no light on the *nature* of the state of affairs. Callon (1986) focuses on the power relationships of actors as they try to impose their views of the world on others (Callon 1986, p.196) or the specific situation at stake. Though these views could be of interest to comparative education and education policy, the comparability of these international studies is limited to comparisons of situations (state of affairs) but cannot delve into their nature (the whys and wherefores). Dale (2006) and Bruner (1996, p.118) define a sense of the state of affairs or situation. Popkewitz (1996), Steiner-Khamsi (2003, 2004), Phillips (1989), and Phillips & Ochs (2003, 2004) go into the intricacies of borrowing and lending. O'Neill (1995) and Carter & O'Neill (1995) cover the hurdles of implementation. Spillane (2004) investigates the world of shifting meanings in sensemaking. Lindblad & Popkewitz (2004b), and Czarniawska and Sevón (1996, 2005) look into traveling policies, translations and narratives. All of them focus their attention on the nature of change or on the processes that try to explain why and how the state of affairs came about or why and how situations change over time.

Studies such as PISA can report on the state of affairs and determine levels or ranking of performance of 15-year-old students, but they cannot make claims about the nature of the state of affairs – why, how, what, who, when and for whom? This notion or finding is of fundamental value to the studies of comparative and international education.

Decentralization and School Autonomy

From the methodological point of view my research is about system-level policies – the macro or national unit of analysis. I look at the institutions and the incentives for change in schools, rather than at schools, classrooms and pedagogical theories or practices themselves. So my study falls within the bounds of comparative education as defined by Halls (1977, p.82) and not under comparative pedagogy as defined by Halls (1977, pp.81-82) and, in more detail, by Alexander (2001).

Decentralization and autonomy are related topics but they are by no means the same thing. The findings of my research add perception-based data to the understanding of comparative, international and policy-borrowing phenomena. Should the world be diverging rather than converging, borrowing or lending may be attempted but never really realized. In a world of divergence, borrowing policies may translate into huge social debts or fiascoes, as the examples of the spread of science policies and lifelong learning ideas from Finnemore (1993) and Jakobi (2006) suggest.

My research adds some evidence to the literature that sees the world of education policies, processes and practices as a world with more diversity than unity and demonstrating more complexity than simplicity. This is not the first study that finds evidence of divergence rather than convergence. Empirically, Astiz et al (2002) argue that even with the globalization force behind national education, systems have not responded with synchronized reforms: "Globalization does not necessarily produce simple isomorphism . . ." (p.87).

And yet, policy convergence may be happening at the labeling of policies or policy ideas or very broad pedagogical definitions (Alexander 2001). However, as we try to get those labels or ideas down to schools, principals, teachers and students, their meaning and scope change or diverge among systems and across time. Again it's a case of elements being lost in translation (Steiner-Khamsi 2004; Phillips 1989) or implementation (Spillane 2004; O'Neill 1995; Dyer 1999), or being changed by the translators or imposing actors (Latour 1986, 2005; Callon 1986; Law 1986).

One of the ideas that became a fad and a buzzword during the last twenty years of the last century was the idea of devolution of power to schools. The fashion of the time favored decentralization of decision-making over centralization, and more autonomy in schools over less autonomy. Evidence of policy changes across countries (Astiz et al 2002) suggests a recent shift back to recentralization[5] of some of the decision-making powers that international organizations so eagerly promoted and all types of governments (democratic, autocratic, parliamentary, presidential, centralized, decentralized) imported for almost twenty years, as documented below. What seems to be true is that decentralization of education policies were designed and implemented in tandem with centralization or recentralization measures. At best, what we observe is a mixture of decentralization and centralization policies.

Evidence of convergence can be found in the language, rhetorical or diffusion realms. There is no evidence that the 'ideas' were translated into policies and practices that meant the same thing across systems. Concepts such as decentralization and autonomy or marketization and accountability are too broad and too abstract to merit any coherent comparative analysis in practical or theoretical terms from one country to another or one system to another.

Translating or transferring concepts, ideas or policies subject to many different meanings or interpretations may prove disappointing from the policy point of view. Lending or borrowing concepts or ideas in the name of autonomy, decentralization and accountability may seriously compromise the running of institutions and raise questions about the applicability of the "solutions". Lending policies from a supply-driven perspective rather than from an inside-outwards or demand-driven movement (in the sense of an idea nationally and historically supported) may also have unintended consequences. Finnemore (1993) ridicules this supply-led approach by citing the 'science policy' trend propelled by an epistemic community of policy-makers at UNESCO. Simply lending policies to developing countries from elsewhere is not wise. The attempt to transfer the science policies of world powers such as the US, the UK, or France to developing countries from Asia, Africa or Latin America (Finnemore 1993) resulted in the establishment of bureaucracies and agencies of science and technology policy in places where there was no scientific community and no need for one. The only need that was met was that of the epistemic community at work.

Students of decentralization policies in education have approached

---

[5] In 1994 Dale saw this policy dialectic between decentralization and centralization in the center of the decentralization movement: '. . . apparently contradictory phenomenon of simultaneous decentralisation and centralisation that seems to be found in many contemporary education systems' (Dale 1994, p.254).

the issue from their own perspective. Few writers have viewed the Mexican case in a comparative way. So to understand the forces behind decentralization and the concept of decentralization with an international and comparative perspective, I drew on the ideas and findings of studies of decentralization done elsewhere. This helped me to develop the idea that decentralization, as understood and implemented by education systems, has different meanings (Crossley & Watson 2003, p.42).

The Different Meanings of Decentralization or Devolution of Power and Autonomy

The first difficulty is with the meaning of decentralization. In general terms for the lay public decentralization may have many meanings.

> The words *centralization* and *decentralization* can mean different things to different people (Bray 2003, p.205).

> 'Decentralisation' is an umbrella word that shelters a number of meanings . . . . Indeed, there is a cluster of words often employed interchangeably in everyday discourse: decentralisation, delegation, devolution, deconcentration, dispersal (Boston et al., p.163).

Different reform policies have been labeled as decentralization (Gershberg 1999 p.63) too. Decentralization may mean the extent to which a central authority designs and implements decisions. It could also mean the degree of freedom or autonomy a school, the principal and the teachers actually have when making and implementing decisions.

Along with the different meanings of decentralization, we find related concepts such as governance, autonomy and site-based management that make the whole inquiry into the literature of state-society relations (Popkewitz 1996, p.27) very difficult to track.

Furthermore, decentralization, autonomy, marketization and privatization are buzzwords for reform and restructuring of education systems. They may come together in a package of reforms but they mean different things.

> In a variety of national contexts, there have been discussions about the changing relations of state to the educational arena. Often, these discussions centre on issues concerning the centralization and decentralization of the state or the devolution of power, the latter referring to shifts in the loci of power to geographically local contexts, for example, through community governance of education . . . . At a different level are discussions about 'privatization'

and 'marketization' of social policy, concepts which indicate a major change in the relation of the state to civil society (Popkewitz 1996, p.27).

I concentrate on the issues, policies or ideas of decentralization and autonomy, although privatization and marketization are buzzwords or concepts related to the former.

Over the past two decades, many countries have been engaged in a shift of decision-making authority to lower administrative levels, either to local or regional governments, or to schools. This move towards decentralisation is a global phenomenon, affecting developing as well as industrialised countries, although the motives and incentives are diverse. The increased attention for decentralisation in education is perhaps best reflected by the numerous initiatives to stimulate decision making by schools, such as site- or school-based management (SBM), the local management of schools and the establishment of relatively autonomous schools like the charter schools in the United States. This widespread trend towards school autonomy has also stimulated the debate about the advantages and disadvantages of private schooling. These debates are inspired by micro-economic theory and ideas about the application of market mechanisms such as choice and competition in education (OECD 2005b, p.64).

There is little doubt that decentralization and autonomy for schools were two of the most important policy or system shifts in most education systems (Gibton, Sabar & Goldring, 2000 p.193). International organizations promoted decentralization (Gershberg 1999, p.63; McGinn & Street 1986, p.471; Torres 2003, p.301) and national governments implemented it (Andreas 2006a, p.285; Ross et al 2006, pp.319-320). As Keith Watson (2000, p.48) stated:

One of the main areas of reform in many countries during the past 15 years or so has been that of educational decentralization. While this has become a key feature of many governments' stated educational policy, it is a central plank of major international efforts at restructuring education in transitional, transformational and reconstructing societies.

Bray and Mukundan wrote in their opening paragraph in 2003[6]:

> In all parts of the world, recent decades have brought numerous
> political and administrative reforms in the education sector. A
> considerable proportion of these reforms bear the label of
> decentralisation. Indeed decentralisation has almost become a
> mantra among policy makers and international agencies. These
> individuals and bodies commonly assert that decentralisation can
> facilitate better management and governance of education, and, in
> turn, improve efficiency and enhance relevance.

Many writers[7] have talked about decentralization as one of the most
important features of the movement towards the restructuring of
education systems around the world (Green 1997, Lindblad &
Popkewitz 2004, p.vii; Astiz et al 2002). However, to see if decentralization really is or was a universal trend, as claimed by Fiske
("Decentralization of schools is truly a global phenomenon."1996, p.v)
and by Bray and Mukundan (2003), we have to understand the meaning
of the idea or concept labeled decentralization.

The promotion of decentralization was a fad[8] in education policy

---

[6] Document downloaded from the UNESCO portal without page numbers. The
citation may be found at the first paragraph in the introduction section.

[7] The list of writers who have seen decentralization as an important policy shift
or phenomenon in education or school restructuring is long. Consider the
following: Gershberg, 1999 (world, Mexico and Nicaragua), van Langen,
2001 (Western countries and Netherlands), Tatto, 1999 (Mexico), van Haecht,
2001 (Great Britain, France and Scandinavian countries), McGinn and Street,
1986 (Peru, Chile and Mexico), Gibton, Sabar and Goldring, 2000 (world and
Israel), Watson, K., 2000 (world), Bray and Mukundan, 2003 (world),
Mukundan and Bray, 2004 (India and world), van Amelsvoort and Scheerens,
1997 (Europe).

[8] This trend towards decentralization also reached Latin America. As a senior
economist from the World Bank states, 'Latin America presents a variety of
experiences in the decentralization of education. Practically all countries have
undertaken some form of decentralization of their education system, which
involved the transfer of decision making autonomy to actors within
("deconcentrated" bodies). . .' (di Gropello 2004, p.2). Evidence of this trend
may be also found, among many others, in Gershberg 1999; Tatto, 1999;
McGinn and Street, 1986; Kaufman and Nelson, 2005; Faletti 2001
(Argentina); Cuéllar-Marchelli, 2002 (El Salvador). Evidence of the trend
toward decentralization with the influence of international organizations such
as the World Bank may also be found in Torres (2003, p.305) and Arnove et al.
(1997, pp.146-147).

change and restructuring, but whether countries around the world implemented decentralization or finally adopted it successfully is another matter. Even the World Bank[9] actively promoted decentralization (World Bank 1995, 1999; Bray & Mukundan 2003), as did the International Monetary Fund (IMF) (Alexander 2000). Other organizations such as the OECD hinted at decentralization too. The head of the Indicators and Analysis Division of the OECD responsible for the PISA project described it as a significant policy tool to bring about improvements in educational performance at school level (Schleicher 2006a, p.285). The ten mandates from the Washington Consensus (Williamson 1993) were so strong that they reached the arena of education in the forms of marketization, competition and decentralization.

By the turn of the century the promotion of decentralization or devolution of power had begun to fade, albeit at a slow pace. A linguistic shift towards new hyphenated buzzwords, 'decentralization-recentralization', 'decentralization-accountability' and 'decentralization-standardization' can be seen in the publications of the World Bank (1999, 2004a, 2004b) or World Bank-related publications (di Gropello 2004).

The literature on decentralization (devolution of decision-making) is vast as there are several significant works dealing with the realm of schools and site-based management. This ranges from the literature on school improvement and effectiveness, and on school reform, to the literature on site-based management and autonomy of decision-making in schools. The literature also increases significantly when experts in public policy or public management write about decentralization of decision-making in education.

However, the literature on decentralization of education with a comparative perspective in Mexico is sparse. I know of only two attempts to classify education systems from the decentralization perspective that refer to Mexico: one conducted by Rideout and Ural (1993, cited by Bray 2003, p.211) and the other covered by the OECD in several publications that I refer to later in greater detail. A study that Gonnie van Amelsvoort and Jaap Scheerens (1997) conducted in some European countries is of relevance since the methodology is the same as

---

[9]   The following paragraph, from a 1999 World Bank publication (1999b, p.50), highlights the importance of decentralization to the World Bank. 'The Bank's Top Education Priorities in the Region . . . *Making decentralization work* by re-engineering education ministries, supporting governance reforms and improvements in information that ensure accountability, and assisting countries in identifying changes in incentives that could alter the behavior of providers and affect the sustainability of reform initiatives.' [Original italics]

the one used by the OECD for the classification of educational systems according to the degree of devolution of decision-making and schools' autonomy. To try to understand the meaning of decentralization and autonomy of schools and their relationship to a best practice model, I too classified education systems in terms of decentralization and autonomy of schools as perceived by principals, teachers and experts.

From examining the perception-based data of the experts and practitioners surveyed in my study, I make some suggestions on the relationship of decentralization and autonomy to a best practice model. If the world is converging, the policies and practices in school education systems and pedagogies, in Alexander's terms (2000, 2001), should look similar. Otherwise, the reality of the situation is divergence.

The research data enabled a comparison of each country to the rest of the countries respectively in the sample but also to an aggregated observation that I have called rest of the world (RW). Looking at specific meanings of words and policies, I have found some evidence that seems to reinforce the hypothesis of a world explained by divergence rather than convergence in policies, processes and practices – except for some specific traits or features (inputs and some outputs) as later explained. My classification of decentralization of decision-making follows the definition of decision-making power as 'territorial centralization/decentralization', as proposed by Bray (2003, p.205).

There is ample evidence to support the view that in the world of education forces are concurrently converging and diverging. Convergence is seen in slogans, signs and broad definitions or practices mainly in inputs and outputs. This includes not only the inputs and outputs cited by Meyer et al (1997), but also convergence in teaching and learning, as suggested by Alexander (2000, 2001). Divergence is seen in meanings, policies, processes and practices (see Table 5.1). However, delving into the more specific interpretations of policy drivers such as centralization and decentralization, or the comparability of international studies such as PISA and TIMSS, or the transferability of policies, processes and practices, reality seems to be explained more by diversity than by similarity.

In models where a federal system of education defines devolution of power to the states or provinces, localities or districts – such as the Canadian, US or Swiss systems – the system is territorially, federally and nationally less centralized, at least in theory. This does not necessarily mean that the schools have the power of decision-making or autonomy. It may mean that the power of decision-making is located at a different level of governmental authority but not within the walls of the schools. It may also mean that the schools have the power of decision-making over key features or aspects of school education. So, in terms of the distribution of power between an authority and the school, only the location of power has changed – in one case at national or federal level and in the other at state or local level. For the school and from the school's point of view the level of the external authority is meaningless as long as this external authority has the power of decision-making over the school.

There are some strange anomalies. It can happen that in a federally decentralized system such as in Canada or the US, the local or provincial authorities exert considerable power over the schools so that, from the school's point of view, the devolution of power has not reached them. Another scenario is that in a relatively centralized education system schools see themselves with considerable autonomy as is the case in New Zealand, as documented later.

When I finally conducted my interviews and issued questionnaires to principals, teachers and experts, the topics of decentralization and autonomy of schools needed much discussion. My question: "How centralized/decentralized is education policy in your country?" was answered cautiously: "It all depends . . ." The reason for this reservation became clear. For countries with very specific regional distribution of power, such as the US, Canada or Switzerland, the question was then divided into two further questions – one for the country and one for the district, province or region. For countries with very different systems such as Great Britain (England and Scotland) and Belgium (Flanders), the question was phrased with only one meaning, namely country and region. In the Bray and Thomas (1995) sense they are the same unit of analysis or observation. This is why the presentation of the findings are divided into two categories, namely country and region – where region refers to state or provincial governments such as Flanders in Belgium or Boston in Massachusetts. The most accurate and most comparable data is provided at the regional level. However, for countries such as Mexico or France, with very large and centralized education systems, the whole meaning of decentralization is straight forward: there are not regions or districts with decentralized systems in the same sense as in the U.S., Canada or Switzerland. In Mexico and France devolving power to the states or provinces would be seen as an aggressive move towards decentralization.

Making comparisons across these systems is quite painful and has to be done with circumspection. Further to Halls' opinion that "comparative studies in education are about the business of comparing what is comparable" (1977, p.81), one could say that comparative education is a field in or approach to education where suggestions can be made to show that some elements are not comparable; they cannot be compared and cannot, therefore, be borrowed, lent or transferred.

To complicate things even further, many of the studies on decentralization of education have not been written from an international or comparative perspective. They have been documented using a national or domestic level of analysis or perspective only.

Whatever the meaning of decentralization, such policies were often associated with new public management, neo-liberalism (Gershberg 1999, p.99) and new responses to globalization (Astiz et al 2002.).

Dale, who is not always identified with the epistemic community of borrowing, lending and translation, wrote:

> However, there has been little investigation of the precise mechanisms of these schemes and it frequently appears to be assumed that what is 'privatization' or 'decentralization' in one country is the same in another. Recognizing though that education systems have nowhere (with the possible exception of Chile) [not in my opinion a good example] literally been privatized, and that there are numerous and very different possible interpretations of decentralization, delegation, devolution, and so on, should give us pause before assuming that we are talking about the same phenomenon (Dale 1997, p.273).

New research in the area has borne out Dale's conjecture. In order to offer some evidence as to how different systems arrive at decentralization for totally different reasons and also define decentralization in different ways, I consider the decentralization of school education systems in Mexico, New Zealand, the US and Singapore. In Chapters 3 and 4, I use the data collected from my research to offer some additional non-representative evidence for the lack of convergence in education policies and education systems, and, therefore, the difficulties of tying performance to a best practice model.

Mexico

While most of the research on education decentralization and school autonomy in Mexico is policy-based (McGuinn & Street 1986 and Tatto 1999), politically based (Grindle 2002, 2006, McGuinn & Street 1986, Posner 2002) or historically based (Arnaut 1998), the non-policy-based literature is descriptive only. Very few works fall within the comparative and international education framework. However, in the paper by McGinn and Street (1986) the authors compare three decentralization policy cases in Latin America, namely Chile, Peru and Mexico. From these narrative comparisons they arrive at the conclusion that changes in education policies are a function primarily of policy-makers' preferences, in other words the state's preferences. There is no real democratic participation in some of these countries. As long as decentralization policies benefit groups that serve the interests of the ruling group, policy-makers from non-democratic, non-pluralist societies will decentralize. Their decentralization policies are not genuine.

Genuine decentralization or participation of all the people first requires the achievement of consensus at least about the value of widespread participation. This can be achieved in a pluralist society, that is, one in which there exist strong groups with projects different from those of the state. However, it cannot be achieved or at least maintained for long, in a society with marked social divisions that deny some groups access to the resources necessary to achieve their objectives. A strong state must first achieve some minimal degree of social equity so that decentralization can lead to genuine participation (McGinn & Street, 1986, p.490).

Despite the conclusions that seem to be in line with the politics of Mexican decentralization policies in education, their analysis does not fall within the ambit of my research. The McGinn and Street study covers the extent to which high-performing countries homogeneously adopt decentralization policies, the degree of comparability of these decentralization policies and whether the meaning of decentralization for decision-making is the same across these countries. Only in the sense that the article compares education policies is it similar to my research. It is important to note that McGinn and Street's paper was published in 1986, five-and-a-half years before the largest education modernization/decentralization policy ever was designed and implemented in Mexico. In May 1993 the national government issued a new modernization and decentralization policy in the guise of an accord known as ANMEB[10] (National Understanding for the Modernization of School Education in Mexico). This understanding was presented as a social understanding with all social groups or organizations directly or indirectly involved in education, from the national union of teachers *(Sindicato Nacional de Trabajadores de la Educación*, SNTE) to the governors of the 31 states of Mexico, business organizations, and even

---

[10] ANMEB stands for *Acuerdo Nacional para la Modernización de la Educación Básica*, the biggest and most recent attempt by Mexican authorities to decentralize the education system and education policy-making.

church leaders. The analysis of the politics and law of the decentralization (Andere, 2006) of education policy in Mexico shows that the decentralization was a political act rather than a real policy shift (see also Andere 2007). In effect the federal government gave more power to the SNTE and kept the really substantial issues of school education policy at the center within its own confines. Since then policies of decentralization to states and schools have been limited to political declarations and rhetorical legitimizing. McGinn and Street were correct in their conclusions even eight years before the ANMEB decentralization in 1993.

In a more recent article, Posner (2002) raises the issue of the risks and difficulties of educational policy change in the transition from a corporativist system under a corporativist state (with a ruling party) to a liberal democracy (p.401). Although the paper does not concentrate solely on policy matters such as the decentralization of decision-making and devolution of power to states and schools, he describes a system where the state and its ruling class keep and control decision-making:

> The history of Mexico, from its political revolution of 1910 until recent times, is an example of a system and practice of education which emphasizes control and in which the middle class never enjoyed relative independence, being beholden to the system itself for its continued existence.

What is relevant to my research from Posner's exploratory analysis is the observation that for some reason the research on topics related to education policy is limited, as I pointed out at the beginning of this section. When the topic of research pertains to education decentralization and devolution of policies (Posner 2002 pp.403, 412), there is even less material.

Gershberg (1999), Ornelas (1998), Andere (2003, 2006, 2007), Tatto (1999), Guevera (2006), McGinn and Street (1986) and others have outlined the reasons for not being able to use Mexico as an example of real decentralization, despite claims from politicians and policy-makers to the contrary. In Mexico the 'slogan'[11] of modernization and decentralization of education appeared to mutate into recentralization of decision-making, but in different ways. From the work of Astiz et al (2002) we know that there is no evidence for a strong direct relationship between globalization and decentralization. My study adds evidence to

---

[11] O'Neill (p.1) uses the word 'slogan' to illustrate that reform or change in education might mean different things to different people.

the lack of convergence of school education and therefore to the limitations of international studies when making claims about comparisons in policies, processes and practices under a best practice model.

Tatto claims that "the rhetoric of the reform includes talk about improving education to move the country towards a global economy and a growing democratic and technological society" (1999, p.259). However, in the wording of ANMEB I did not find a single direct reference to the 'global economy' – or global threat or global society or even to the word 'global.'[12] The people who drafted the most important document to reform education in Mexico were not thinking in terms of the relationship between education and globalization. From this public and most important document (ANMEB), it was not clear whether education was seen as a response to the challenges of globalization or if it was an action to move the country towards the desirable objective of a global economy. Whatever the relationship, the policy-makers' view of education resulted in a plan of modernization and deconcentration, or decentralization. The drafters of ANMEB used the following argument for launching the reform:

> There exists a clear *consensus* about the need to transform the education system in Mexico. This social claim, spread not only geographically across the whole country but also among all sectors of society, is a call for quality in education. (Zedillo et al 1992, p.3) [My translation; my italics]

However, the drafters of the document provided no evidence of such consensus. There is in fact some evidence to the contrary (Andere, 2006). Parents and teachers, at least, seemed to be satisfied with the quality of school education in Mexico. They were content at the beginning of the 1990s and they remained pleased with the system at the beginning of the 2000s. The drafters went even further, claiming that there was 'wide consensus' (Zedillo et al 1992, pp.12, 15) on the need to implement curriculum changes both in primary or elementary education and lower secondary education. Again, the policy-makers or drafters of ANMEB provided no evidence of such 'wide consensus.'

There is no evidence that the territorial decentralization in Mexico was a reaction to a global threat, nor that it actually materialized into real decentralization or reduction of control (Tatto 1999, p.280) of the

---

[12] Contrary to what Tatto says (p.560), President Salinas did not technically sign the ANMEB. His signature was only 'ornamental' under the heading of 'witness.'

central government in the most important components of education policy. After ANMEB, central control was reaffirmed and increased (Andere 2006, p.48). What it boiled down to was that the decentralization meant more work for states though not more power in terms of decision-making. The management of buildings and the teachers' payroll were transferred to the states. The central government kept control of the core curriculum, labor policies and school schedules. The Mexican case is an example of 'reform-talk' or 'sloganized' reform.

The instrumentalist hypothesis of politics and decision-making may explain decentralization of education in Mexico. In some developing countries decentralization appears to be instrumental to the center's conservation of power (McGinn & Street 1986, p.472). This instrumentalist approach ties in well with non-democratic and non-pluralistic countries (McGinn & Street 1986). In these regimes decentralization policies are carried out only if they are deemed politically correct and instrumental to the control of power by those who already control power. According to these authors, external forces do not explain decentralization of education in Mexico. They maintain that the external-forces hypothesis is less convincing than that of internal political forces and idiosyncrasies. They bounce between perceptions and ideas of what works and the political considerations of what is convenient for politicians, policy-makers and interest groups.

New Zealand

A good example of radical decentralization is New Zealand. New Zealand's decentralization and new public management took place in a radical (Boston et al 1996) and broad way (Dale 2001, p.496). Education reform was part of a comprehensive new public management approach, with three main reasons provided as justification: perceived poor educational outcomes, deficiencies in educational administration and preparing New Zealand to participate fully in an internationally competitive economy and society (Boston et al 1996, p.171). According to the Education Review Office (as cited by Boston et al 1996, p.172):

> The aim . . . was to be achieved by altering the incentive structure within the administration of education through two major structural changes. The first was to abolish all layers of administration between the central state agencies and the local school in order to locate decision making as close as possible to the point of implementation and thereby achieve greater administrative efficiency and responsiveness.

The second was to alter the balance of power between the providers and the clients of education by providing communities with the means for a greater say in the running of their schools and for expressing their expectations about children's education.

By some standards, and certainly in the Mexican view, this method of decentralizing in New Zealand would be seen as a move towards centralization of authority rather than one of decentralization. This is because local or provincial intermediaries were eliminated. According to Boston et al (1996, p.172), the result is that the New Zealand education system has collapsed between the two new stakeholders, the Ministry of Education and the parent-elected board of education in each school. This is why, as is shown later, the responses I received from interviewees in New Zealand were located at the very left end of a centralization–decentralization continuum. This is an interesting outcome for a country that is seen as highly decentralized after the Tomorrow's Schools initiative of 1989 that reformed the school education system in favor of more school autonomy.

Decentralization in New Zealand meant centralization by different forces and logic. In both cases, Mexico and New Zealand, the slogan of decentralization was used and meant more control by the central authority. Yet the reforms in Mexico and New Zealand have nothing in common. In New Zealand, even with more power of decision-making at the national or central government level, autonomy of schools was increased dramatically. In Mexico no autonomy to schools or devolution of decision-making ever occurred. In New Zealand schools are autonomous since school boards are entrusted with managing the schools directly. There is no intervention from a local authority or government representation on parental school boards. The perception-based data of my study confirms this autonomy where New Zealand is located to the right of the less-autonomy–more-autonomy continuum. In Mexico independent decision-making school boards do not even exist for government schools.

It is not clear whether the drive towards decentralization in New Zealand was decided after promotion by or interaction with international organizations, or as a reaction to it. Analysis and data seem to point to the view that a 'dialect' occurred between international and national actors when the system was being designed and implemented (Dale 2001, p.496).

United States
Not all accounts of decentralization are as well defined, packaged or

strategically designed as in Mexico and New Zealand. The United States provides a completely different example. The pressure for independence between schools and city governments came from grassroots level and civic organizations rather than epistemic communities from government or academia (Gittell 1972). The movement originated at the people's level (Kaufman 1969, p.6). Boards of Education in America were meant to channel public participation in schools (Gittell 1972, p.670). They were not the bureaucratic design of a group of people in the policy-making ranks advised by academics or international organization communities.

> The local board of education was designed to be the primary means of citizen participation in school policy making (Gittell 1972, p.670).

School governance and decentralization in the US continued to evolve towards more community control of schools (Gittell 1972, p.677). Only in recent years have there been increasing strikes against the tradition of local community control of schools. One of those strikes originated from efforts towards standardization across the world and the US. This is another movement that has not yet converged on the high-performing countries and has apparently been adopted by other countries such as Mexico.[13]

One statistic often cited as an indication of centralization in education policy in the US is the sharp decline in the number of school districts from a total of 117,108 in 1939-40 to a total of 14,383 in 2003-4 (National Center for Education Statistics, 2001). More recently, the No Child Left Behind Act (NCLBA)[14] has challenged the decentralization tradition with more federal intervention through a strategic web of goals, rules and monetary incentives. Nonetheless, and at least until

---

[13] On February 9, 2006 the Secretary of Education in Mexico revealed a plan to test all Mexican students during different stages in primary and lower secondary schools (*Comunicación* Social*, 2006).

[14] 'On January 8, 2002, President Bush signed into law the No Child Left Behind Act of 2001 (NCLBA). This law represents his education reform plan and contains the most sweeping changes to the Elementary and Secondary Education Act (ESEA) since it was enacted in 1965. It changes the federal government's role in education, from kindergarten through 12th grade, by requiring America's schools to describe their success in terms of what each student accomplishes.' (Rhode Island Parent Information Network. Retrieved on November 20, 2006 from http://www.ripin.org/nochildleftbehind.html.)

the beginning of the new century, decentralization of education in the US has been a battle fought and won at street or community level rather than as a reaction to external forces such as globalization or competition. In Mexico and New Zealand, established epistemic communities generated devolution-of-power ideas with a top-down designed plan without 'street fights.' In none of these cases (that of Mexico, New Zealand or the US) can the influence of external forces or the promotion of international intermediaries explain the changes. International intermediaries may have been present, but there is no clear, unambiguous proof that national authorities reacted to this 'pressure' rather than reacting to a 'rational' drive for improvement (as in New Zealand) or to a 'rational' drive for political accommodation and enhancement of the ruling elite (as in Mexico).

Singapore

At first glance education policies in Singapore seem very modern and westernized. However, a more thorough investigation (for example, Professor Gopinathan's account, as discussed in the first chapter, and my observations and some of my interviews) reveals a more complex picture. A very powerful, centralized, yet effective, government designs, organizes and dictates policies and practices involving education in Singapore. The answers that I received from the few people that I was able to interview were synchronized, leading to the belief that the system is orchestrated and, moreover, that there are specific directives that people were expected to follow. The current one (2006) is 'creativity.' Policy-makers, experts, principals and teachers talked about the creativity drive; changes in curriculum and schools are made in the belief that they will encourage students to be more creative. The merit-driven school system has been made more flexible to create a talent-driven system – a slogan that reflects this change is: 'Think out of the box.' However, notions of creativity are passed to the schools, principals and teachers like some kind of recipe. As one interviewee (from elsewhere) told me, 'It's like the policy-makers ordered the schools and students to be creative.'

If we do not have the history or the context, we cannot understand the real meaning of policies. In Singapore decisions simulate markets, decentralization, autonomy and competition – decisions made at the top are followed by all in the middle and at the bottom. Catchy slogans such as "Thinking Schools, Learning Nation" or "Teach Less, Learn More" are used to implement decisions so that they can easily filter down to society and so that all can march to the same beat. In Singapore decentralization and marketization occur at the levels of slogans and simulation – and their labels – rather than as any real devolution of power or concept of autonomy.

The Role of International Organizations

From the analysis of the four cases, it is clear that by different means and resources national or federal states remain powerful in education. Whether in a large, federal, and centrally controlled system such as Mexico, or in a small nationally monolithic system, democratic such as New Zealand, or autocratic such as Singapore, or a large federal and yet state-controlled system such as the United States, the power remains with the state. According to Roger Dale, at least in Europe and the European Union, the power of states to develop common educational policies, especially at the higher education level, may be fading.[15] The rescaling and redistribution of power among local, regional, national and global entities may explain this (Robertson 2006a, 2006b). This transnationalism or supranationalism does not seem to be pervading other regions of the world. When states have power over their education systems, whether in a federal or national system of education, they exercise power by means of curriculum, standards and examinations or by means of incentives, as occurs in the US. The closest one gets to the mundialization of school education policies and practices is in the borrowing/lending practices of ideas and policies that international organizations promote. Even in this respect, a world of supranational structures and regulatory frameworks is far from reality.

A lot of real change in governmental policies in education at the national level has occurred. The literature on the influence of globalization and traveling policies is huge – even if the intention in adopting these ideas seems to be to legitimize the rhetoric (van Haecht, p.69.) International organizations such as the OECD, UNESCO, the World Bank and the governments behind them have influenced the new research.

Jullien's dream of compiled and organized data facilitated comparative research into education systems (as cited by Crossley & Watson 2003, pp.34-35) when international organizations such as UNESCO, the World Bank and the OECD started to accumulate large and standardized data sets (Crossley & Watson 2003, p.35). A brief review of publications from UNESCO, the World Bank, the OECD and the IEA's sponsored assessments tells a very eloquent story about the improvements in data-gathering and data-sharing. PISA and TIMSS in mathematics and science and PISA and PIRLS in reading offer a mine of

---

[15] Point raised by Prof. R. Dale during a personal interview in his office at Bristol University on April 4, 2006.

normalized or standardized information that facilitates some comparisons. However, the facilitation of comparisons by the abundance of information could take comparability to the extreme. Information provided in aggregated and standardized data sets can lead to shallow or insufficient analysis, as Crossley and Watson (2003, p.35) warn, and as I try to document here.

Many kinds of relations and comparisons are drawn from international studies such as PISA and TIMSS. The secretariats of the organizations responsible for PISA and TIMSS, with the help of international networks and teams, do not restrict their task to the release and publication of results. They make claims about education policies and practices by comparing the results of assessments and relating them to policies, practices and even features of education systems and organizations. In some policy recommendations they try to transfer a best practice model.

One such case is the OECD's comparative study of national systems and policies of education as applied to centralization/ decentralization of decision-making and school autonomy. The direct predecessors of my research are the analysis of centralization/ decentralization of making decisions and the classification derived from it. Apart from being inductive and comparative in nature, the end result of both the OECD's study and mine is the location of patterns, the ordering of tendencies and the categorization of education systems and policies into certain criteria. I turn next to this.

3

The Views of International Organizations on Decentralization and Autonomy

There is little to say about decentralization and autonomy in comparative and international education without referring to the ideas and proposals of international organizations. This chapter deals with the role of international organizations and some of their proposals in decentralization and autonomy. I also present the views of the OECD. Finally, I compare the OECD's studies and proposals with my own research findings.

International organizations have tried to play a part in shaping new policies in education (Watson, K. 1996, p.213). Whether they have been effective or not is another matter. Since international organizations are seen as key factors in the interaction between a world of global culture or global forces (globalization or competition) and national education systems, the relationship of these interactions to decentralization of decision-making and autonomy of schools needs further study. International organizations have keenly promoted a best practice model of school education based on decentralization and autonomy. In attempting to demystify the belief in best practice or ideal model, my first aim is to show that if international organizations were indeed promoting an ideal model it was never really realized.

The international organizations and their governmental sponsors have their own agendas for promoting change in education systems. They make specific recommendations on the basic shapes of national education systems. They act as intermediaries between global systemic changes such as economic forces, distribution of labor, world economic order, competition, globalization and national states. In one extreme view, changes at home are explained by looking at changes abroad:

> World-systems analysis restores the international dimension to the field of comparative and international education. It provides a framework that is essential to an understanding of educational developments and reforms . . . that are simultaneously sweeping many of the countries of the world (Arnove 1980, p.62).

The inference is that international factors, forces and ideas affect wider society as they move into new territories by different means or mechanisms. See for example, Dale's "typology of mechanisms of external effects on national policies" (1999, p.6).

At the other extreme, international factors and international organizations have not shaped national policies and practices according to one basic pattern, and policies and practices have not converged. Experts from different epistemic groups accept the influence of international forces such as globalization, as well as the mediation of international organizations. Dale (2000) describes and summarizes the relationships between international organizations, globalization and education policy. He discusses two approaches to the theory of the influence of supranational forces or international organizations exerted upon national education systems: the Common World Educational Culture (CWEC) and the Globally Structured Educational Agenda (GSEA).

According to Dale, CWEC or world culture proponents believe that the relationship is causal in nature, stemming from a system of values and beliefs around a 'world culture' (Meyer et al. 1997) of educational systems. The cognitive or scientific value of the world culture triggers this causal relationship and international organizations act as transmitters. Advocates of the world culture approach or CWEC believe that educational practices and policies are transmitted by their own scientific or intrinsic value, while the global agenda approach believes that those practices are a reflection of the well-defined and powerful economic and political forces of capitalism. The GSEA or global agenda proponents also believe that the transmitting agent between globalization and education relies on international organizations (governmental), but for different reasons. The context and history of each nation-state needs to be considered to fully explain the relationship between globalization and education (Dale 2000). The interaction between the institutions of the world culture and the institutions of the nation-state matters.

For CWEC the patterns of world curriculum and mass schooling are a direct consequence of the world culture. For GSEA these are non-homogenous practices: isomorphism of policies, practices and national education institutions is viewed as something that has to be demonstrated (Dale, 2000, p.448). In the world culture approach the nation-states are not obsolete. However, world science, culture, values and beliefs of a rationalist nature drive policies and practices in education. In this view, international organizations such as UNESCO, the World Bank and the OECD (Dale, 2000, p.443) are the agents for the transmission of the system's values into education. For GSEA the issue is much more complicated. Here, the relationship between education and globalization is a function of a complex interaction (dialectical in nature) between international agents, international organizations, and nation-states (national dominant powers). It is an interaction between the epistemic community of international organizations with a specific agenda, by means of support, imposition, diffusion, persuasion or promotion (Dale 1999), and the national policy-makers framed by contextual, historic and institutional forces of national education systems. In both views international organizations are seen as transmitters of values or beliefs.

From the empirical perspective there is evidence of the intentional influence of international organizations in the works of Reimers (2002) and Gershberg (1999) in the specific case of Latin America. There are scholars who even see an almost complete surrender of national policies to international agencies driven by globalization (McGinn 1996, pp.350-351). However, there is not yet evidence for whether the intentional influence has translated into a global best practice educational model.

If a convergence in policies and practices that mean the same thing is found, then this would be evidence not only of the influence of external forces, but also of convergence to a best practice model. However, if policies and practices of high, middle and low-performing countries are not similar in substance, and do not mean the same thing, then the world is better explained by a more complex hypothesis that sees national and local influences as more relevant.

After looking at the descriptive features of decentralization and school autonomy of Mexico, New Zealand, the US and Singapore in Chapter 2, there appears to be no evidence to support convergence in education policies and practices. However, can the lack of convergence in these four cases be generalized to other countries or regions?

Reimers states that in Latin America there seems to be evidence of the influence of international agencies for a 'model' of education emphasizing efficiency and competitiveness (Reimers 2002, pp.57, 59). On the other hand, as Gershberg affirms, "Nearly every country in Latin America has implemented some form of educational decentralization policy" (1999, p.63). As implied by Gershberg, the latter is so widely defined that it could mean anything.

If mass schooling and curriculum homogeneity across the world are the two most widespread (if unexpected) shared practices, a counter-argument would be that the world culture approach has selected two educational practices or outcomes across the world that would have been observed regardless of whether or not we live in a global world. In all nations of the world, whatever the level of development or political ideology, the number of students (absolute and relative) in schools has increased. It is also highly possible that all countries, irrespective of their global or national situation or context, adopt topics such as science and mathematics, which have generally accepted principles and laws, in curricula and contents in a similar way. The law of gravity is the same whether it is taught in Mexico or China; 2+2=4 is a universal truth. There is only the science of mathematics, of physics, of chemistry and of biology respectively. In these sciences, the curricula of all nations and all school districts around the world have to be the same or significantly equal if they teach mathematics, physics and chemistry. However, when it comes to topics or subjects such as language, history, social sciences and the arts, the values and ideologies and idiosyncrasies of each nation or state, or even each local school district or school, in centralized or decentralized systems, play an important role. The proposition in this matter is, therefore, that non-scientifically related curricula will be more local and more contextual, whereas more scientifically related ones will be similar and will look alike across the board. In this narrow case only, the similarity or isomorphism does not stem from global influences, metropolitan hegemonic forces or international politics; it originates from the logic of its own cognitive value of scientific knowledge.

Even at the level of curriculum and other 'simple matters,' King warns of the difficulties of comparisons among systems (1989, p.371):

> In the particular case of comparative education, the record since the 1960s reveals many instances of failure to understand or convey the exact meaning of scholastic terminology, even in such simple matters as enrolments, attendance, teaching and 'guidance'; the curricular or career importance locally of such items as Latin or mathematics; the 'hidden curriculum' actually experienced not merely by the bulk of the school population but by groups or individuals within it; and so on.

My research seeks to add new evidence for the lack of isomorphism in education policies and practices, with specific emphasis on decentralization and autonomy policies. I will show the evidence of my research in tandem with similar studies conducted by the OECD.

The OECD has specifically studied education systems through the influence of decentralization and autonomy policies. The OECD began its incursion into the analysis of education systems in the late 1980s and early 1990s. The first issue of *Education at a Glance* (OECD 1992) identifies the following indicator: "Decision-making characteristics" comprising the following measures: locus of decision-making, decision-making by schools, domains of decision-making, modes of decision-making, and school autonomy in decision-making (OECD 1992, p.13).

Since then the OECD has paid attention to this issue in different studies and publications.

The OECD's Views

There are two different ways that the OECD has gathered information and produced reports in relation to the topics of decentralization and autonomy of schools and school members (school boards, principals, head teachers and teachers). One of the ways is reported in the *Education at a Glance* series. The other is in a fairly new publication (OECD 2005b) with the title, *School Factors Related to Quality and Equity: Results from PISA 2000* or Factors and Quality (F&Q). The two methodologies are based on data gathered from perceptions. However, the perceptions are gathered from two quite different groups and questionnaires. The two studies are presented separately and are not related. I compare the two OECD studies with my own research. The OECD's decision to report on decision-making factors goes back to the late 1980s and early 1990s with the decision being supported by a belief that decentralization and autonomy are factors that have not only spread around the world for the last two decades or so, but are believed to have had an impact on education quality as well.

> Over the past two decades, many countries have been engaged in a shift of decision making authority to lower administrative levels, either to local or regional governments, or to schools. This move towards decentralisation is a global phenomenon, affecting developing as well as industrialised countries, although the motives and incentives are diverse. The increased attention for decentralisation in education is perhaps best reflected by the numerous initiatives to stimulate decision making by schools, such as site- or school-based management (SBM), the local management of schools and the establishment of relatively autonomous schools like the charter schools in the United States. This wide-spread trend towards school autonomy has also stimulated the debate about the advantages and disadvantages of private schooling (OECD 2005b, p.64).

Although the two studies are based on different methodologies and are under the responsibility of different drafting bodies within the Education Directorate at the OECD, they are conducted or framed under the academic auspices of a group of researchers at the University of Twente (Netherlands). Therefore, while some of the language used in these reports is similar, it is difficult to make a direct comparison between them. For instance, in both studies the analysis is made under a theoretic-cal framework of domains and modes and domains and levels that coincide in some aspects but not in others. As a consequence the comparison between the OECD's studies and my own research will be made separately.

Table 3.1 shows in a nutshell the main similarities and differences in the wording and levels of analysis in the two OECD studies.

Table 3.1: The OECD's Decision-making Theoretical Framework

'Education at a Glance'[1]	'Factors and Quality'[2]
Domains	**Domains**
• The organization of instruction	• Curriculum and instruction
• Personnel management	• Personnel management
• Planning and structures	• Student policies
• Resources	• Financial resources
Modes	**Levels**
• In full autonomy	• Elected or appointed school board
• In consultation with others	• The school principal
• Within a framework	• The department head
• Other	• Teachers

Sources:
1. OECD 2004b
2. OECD 2005b

I refer to the meaning and scope of each of the OECD studies separately. Then, I compare the publications (*Education at a Glance* and Factors and Quality) with my own research.

The 'Education at a Glance' View
Chapter 6 of the OECD's *Education at a Glance* 2004 (2004b, pp.423–38) classifies many PISA countries according to a variable called Decision Making in Education Systems (DMES). However, no direct claims are made in this publication about the relationship between DMES and the performance of students or systems.

More recently, two different but related publications (OECD 2005; Guichard 2005) complement the 'neutral' OECD analysis (2004b) and relate DMES to quality performance and efficiency. Guichard (2005, p.16) and the OECD (2005, p.54) maintains in exactly the same words:

> There is a presumption that the devolution of responsibilities to local authorities and schools brings efficiency . . . **Although there is no common model, in most countries that performed well in PISA surveys, local authorities and schools have substantial**

autonomy to adapt educational content and/or allocate and manage resources (this is the case in England, Korea, Finland, Japan and the Netherlands for instance; Australia on the other hand performed above the average at PISA with very little devolution of responsibilities to schools) . . . In Mexico, decisions related to education are taken mostly at the central level by the federal government or the state authorities. **Schools have some autonomy in the organization of instruction, but have no autonomy at all in personnel management and resource allocation, and only very limited autonomy in planning and structure.** Modest steps have been taken to give them more responsibilities The *reforma integral de la secundaria* [integral curriculum reform for lower secondary schools] gives some autonomy to both the States and schools in designing curricula. *Escuelas de calidad* [Quality Schools, a program designed to promote managerial skills in schools] promotes deeper changes in responsibility devolution, including in terms of resources allocation. However, the scope of these programmes is limited both regarding the number of schools that participate and the means. *Overall more progress is needed in terms of devolution to all schools and local authorities, especially as concerns the use of financial resources and staff management. Such devolution requires accompanying measures. First, school principals, whose role should evolve from mainly administrative to a role more focused on improving learning processes, need training. Second, accountability has to increase.* [Original italics in OECD, 2005; no italics in Guichard; my parenthesis and bold, my translations]

There are many issues with the analysis of DMES as a variable and the wording of the quoted paragraph. The *Education at a Glance* (OECD 2004b) analysis of DMES is more descriptive than judgmental. However, the Guichard and Economics Department analysis of DMES is more judgmental than descriptive. The discrepancy may come from the drafters and the views of two different directorates at the OECD. *Education at a Glance* is drafted by the Division of Education Indicators and Analysis within the Directorate of Education, whereas the *Economic Survey for Mexico* is published by the Economic and Development Review Committee and drafted by three people, among them Stéphanie Guichard. One can only assume that the education section of the report was drafted by Guichard since the wording of her article and the OECD's Survey is the same. Thus, whereas the analysis and conclusions of data are written in a less judgmental fashion by the *Education*

at a Glance report (OECD 2004b) than the Survey's report, both documents are published under the aegis of the OECD's management bodies.

Furthermore, the introductory section of the OECD's survey on
Mexico (OECD 2005, p.10) states:

> Over the past decades, Mexico has made great progress in
> increasing school enrolment in a context of tight budgets, rapid
> growth of the school-age population, great linguistic diversity,
> sizeable internal and two-way cross-border migration flows, and a
> high degree of extreme poverty. There has been a deliberate
> increase in public spending on education; but while the volume of
> educational services has increased, there are doubts about whether
> the additional funding is actually delivering the expected improve-
> ments. Both the coverage and quality of education services remain
> far behind OECD **best practices** even though, on paper, average
> teacher-pupil ratios are not out of line. And the system is not able
> to prevent poverty from reproducing itself from one generation to
> the next. Many children, especially the poor ones, still drop out
> before completing compulsory education and school-leavers have
> poor literacy and numerical skills. *Oportunidades* [Opportunities,
> a social policy to reduce poverty] has shown itself to be an effective
> programme in reducing poverty, improving education, nutrition
> and health and reducing drop-out rates. It should continue. Beyond
> that, there is much to be done in improving the quality of outcomes
> and access to higher education. [My parenthesis and bold]

From this paragraph we see that the OECD recognizes that there are
indeed best practices in education policies. From this wording, one could
think that the OECD's system of beliefs and values aligns with the CWEC
view of the world – that there are some values out there, best practices
waiting for national states to adopt them. It follows that, if nation-states
were wise enough to adopt or adapt those policies and practices, their
educational problems or challenges would be solved or overcome.

"Who is taught what, how, by whom, where, when . . ." (Dale
2006, p.190) makes the difference. Alternatively, "we need a surer
sense of what to teach to whom and how to go about teaching it in such
a way that it will make those taught more effective, less alienated , and
better human beings" (Bruner 1996, p.118).

Let us then, test this best practice OECD view of the policy-mix
duo of choice in the 1980s and 1990s i.e., decentralization and autonomy of school management.

I start by comparing my findings with the OECD's as published in the OECD's *Education at a Glance* 2004, Chapter D, Indicator D6 (OECD 2004b).

The OECD's methodology as set out in *Education at a Glance* is both similar to and different from the methodology of my research. It is similar in two respects:

- It is based on analysis of perceptions.
- The results are shown in a method of classification.

However, the OECD's methodology is different in all other respects. It is explained in three different documents: the OECD's *Education at a Glance* 2004, Chapter D, Indicator D6 (OECD 2004b), and in two documents provided by the OECD's Education Secretariat, titled "Indicators of National Education Systems: Locus of Decision-Making Questionnaire" (2003a) (NW C 03-020) and "Data Collection Manual: Decision-Making in Education" 2003b) (NW C 03-019).

Since the early 1990s this method of measuring the devolution of decision-making has been applied on three occasions – in 1992 (OECD 1992), 1998 (OECD 1998) and 2003 (OECD 2004b). However, I refer in detail to the latter published in *Education at a Glance* 2004, since Mexico was included only in this one. By looking at the three reports one can deduce the following:

- The basic framework is the same: modes and domains; decentralization and autonomy. However, the 1992 one is much more modest in its presentation of results, compared with the 1998 and 2004 publications. It contains a brief explanation of the method at the end of the report (OECD 1992, pp.136-137).
- From a methodological point of view, the 1998 and 2003 reports are more similar but, even in this case, comparisons have to be made carefully since the composition of panels of experts changed from 1998 to 2003 (OECD 2004b, p.424).
- The analysis in the last report is much more sophisticated and focuses on public lower secondary schools only.

In the 1992 version of *Education at a Glance*[1] the analysis was shallower

---

[1]   1992 was the first year that *Education at a Glance* was published (OECD 1992, p.5). This is an important threshold date not only for the publication of *Education at a Glance,* but for the decision of the OECD to become more involved with education and comparative education. 'The increased demand for information on education and the need for improved knowledge on the functioning of

in the sense that it gave fewer details and explanations compared with the 1998 and 2003 publications but it was also broader because it included public lower secondary education, primary and upper secondary education schools. Comparisons with private schools were also made. The advantage of the OECD's methodology is that the questionnaire is much more structured and defined along very specific questions (OECD 2003a). Figure 3.1 shows an example:

Figure 3.1: Sample of OECD's questionnaire issued to panelists

P1–1 At what level is it decided what school a child should attend?
If pupils/parents are free to choose the school to attend, tick 'School'
ISCED2
[ ]   Central government
[ ]   State government
[ ]   Provincial/regional authorities or governments
[ ]   Sub-regional or inter-municipal authorities or governments
[ ]   Local authorities or governments
[ ]   School, school board or committee

The disadvantage of the OECD's methodology would be twofold:

• There is no way to ensure that the methodology was consistent across all the participating panels.
• The panelists across countries were not consistent in following the same analysis and the same deliberations.

---

the education system raise many questions not only for data collection but also for the organisation, reporting and collection of the data. These questions led the authorities in the Member countries of the OECD to consider new ways of comparing their education systems. Agreement was reached on the feasibility and utility of developing an international set of indicators that would present in statistical form, key features of the education systems of Member countries' (OECD 1992, p.10). One of those indicators was and still is the decision-making characteristics coined in 1992 (OECD 1992, p.13) or 'Decision making in education systems' as described in 2004 (OECD 2004b, p.423). In 1992 the 'set of international education indicators proposed by the OECD' were grouped in three clusters: 1) costs, resources and school process (where we find the decision-making characteristics); 2) demographic, economic and social context; 3) outcomes of education (OECD 1992, p.13). One has only to look at a copy of *Education at a Glance* from 1992 (148 pages long in two languages – English and French) and compare it with *Education at a Glance* from 2005 (435 pages long, English only, plus technical Annexes, OECD 2005c) to find evidence of the increasing sophistication of statistics in comparative education.

There is no way to confirm whether panels were actually organized as there is no published information about the matter. I tried to get that information for Mexico from the Mexican representative to Network C, but I was told to request the information through the 'appropriate channels.' I then made an official inquiry under the Mexican Freedom of Information Act.[2] On July 3, 2006 the Department of Education replied through the Federal Institute for Access to Public Information (IFAI)[3] as follows: ". . . after an exhaustive search for the requested information as it relates to the names of the persons who took part in the panel that answered the OECD's questionnaire, the information was not located in the files of this agency" – the Mexican Department of Public Education, SEP. However, SEP sent me a copy of the questionnaire as it was answered by one of the panelists (at least so I deduce). The person who answered the questionnaire is a public official working for SEP, presumably one of the experts at the national or federal level of education. It is not clear if this completed questionnaire was the result (through consensus) of the panel's discussions or if it was a draft of their work or the draft of one of the panelists. There appears to be no record of the panel ever meeting, since the completed questionnaire sent to me as an electronic copy through the IFAI electronic portal mentions nothing about the panel's organization or response. Judging from the lack of information, and that the person whose name appears as 'Respondent' in the OECD's questionnaire is the same person who is the representative to the OECD's Network C, one cannot conclude that the panel ever met.

Looking at the answers to the questionnaire shown in Figure 3.1, one can take issue with the response. For example, question one, P1–1 is "At what level is it decided what school a child should attend?" The answer on the completed questionnaire is "School, school board or committee." This is not the correct response. The way the selection is done in schools in Mexico varies from state to state and from district to district. The evasive answer from SEP and the clearly inadequate answer to the questionnaire, as suggested by the previous analysis of question P1–1, may add evidence to the thesis of the absence of consistency in the OECD's methodology.

There is no indication that the OECD audits the procedures from

---

[2] The Mexican name for the Freedom of Information Act is: *Ley Federal de Transparencia y Acceso a la Información Pública Gubernamental* [Federal Law for Transparency and Access to Public Government Information] (www.ifai.org.mx/english_version/fltapgi.htm).

[3] IFAI stands for *Instituto Federal de Acceso a la Información Pública*.

the different participating countries to secure homogeneity in the application of the surveys. There is no way to prove that the OECD's methodology was consistently applied and reported around the world. Nor can we establish whether the panels around the world applied the same criteria and construed the questions in the same way. The multiple-choice answers given to panelists to respond to the questionnaire may also hide important information on the intricacies relating to decisions in schools.

For instance, decisions on admission to schools may be based on multi-level or multiple-people involvement – principals and/or teachers and/or parents and/or local authorities; or principals alone; or principals with the advice of the local education authorities. Decisions of admission may also be affected by the 17 (at least) school organizational structures identified in Chapter 2. Decisions on admission may be based on merit, the grades obtained by students at their previous school. These are therefore 'automatic' decisions. Decisions may be based on nearest to school policies, or siblings in the school, or supply and demand (parental choice as opposed to school choice) or a combination of all or some of the above. Then again, decisions may be taken out of the hands of human discretion and left to a complex software program with many variables taken into account. Decisions about admission may be taken as a result of a last-minute call from a politician or important parent or stakeholder trying to influence the decision of principals. As I learnt during my interviews with principals from around the world, some principals yielded to this kind of pressure while others did not. I did not expect principals to admit to this kind of embarrassment (as it would be in some cultures) in a formal questionnaire or interview, but they did under the assurance of anonymity.

All of these (and maybe more) different ways of doing things were reported by my interviewees when I was trying to make a classification index of admission policies and practices in all the schools I visited. The mix of answers reflects a long and intricate list of options. In some cases the level of admission policies and practices was not only complex but sometimes even untraceable. In many cases principals reported some intervention by 'invisible hands' to try to influence admissions. In some instances, principals were able to resist, but in others they were not. In cases such as those where parental choice is exercised fully under a first-come-first-served basis, principals and school management teams were able to tailor the parents' requests by means of private interviews or proxies between parents and school authorities. If the school authorities see that the school is not an appropriate fit for the applicant, they will suggest to the parents that the child will be better off in a different school or that the child will be happier in a less academically demanding school or that there is a school that is a better or more perfect fit for the child.

There is no way that a multiple-choice questionnaire, answered according to the perceptions of three 'experts' – two governmental and one 'school-related' person, but most probably chosen by a central governmental representative, will report on this complex reality. Therefore, it is even less plausible to make a comparison of decision-making policies and practices among schools, districts, systems or countries based on a flawed means of gathering data. The generality or abstraction of the multiple-choice questions will fail to reveal the intricacies of the differences in their answers and thus many important things will be lost. As a consequence we could receive as decentralization something that is really centralized and as autonomy something that is actually decided in central offices. Many of the matters decided in schools are not written in regulations, manuals or curricula. Much of what happens in schools and school districts depends on the personal and political interactions between schools and local authorities and between principals and super-intendents, education chiefs or school board members. In some districts and schools things may run smoothly, but in different schools in the same districts things may be slapdash and sloppy.

The OECD's panels were intended to be composed of people of the same level and with similar knowledge of their respective education systems. They were labeled 'national experts' – although there is no assurance that experts[4] were really chosen for the project in each country. They were supposed to answer the questionnaire by consensus. However, there is no evidence that the panels were indeed organized using common criteria. There is no evidence that the panels faced the same questions in their own language, with an adequate translation; there is no assurance that the same question was understood by the panelists with the same meaning across systems. In the end the OECD secretariat and the Network C secretariat (University of Twente) worked with inputs that had been put together by many contacts from several countries without ensuring that the methodological assumptions were actually met (no public information being available).

Therefore, to claim a relationship between decentralization or autonomy of schools and more efficiency, as in the OECD's wording, or between policies of lagging countries and best practices, is inexact. We

---

[4] There is also the difficulty with the definition of experts. How does one define an expert?

do not have a model of decentralization and autonomy across systems and beyond boundaries.

The Factors and Quality View

Chapter 5 of the OECD's publication, *School Factors Related to Quality and Equity,* titled "Decentralized Decision Making, Privatization and Student Performance" (OECD 2005b, pp.63-86) deals with decentralization and autonomy with a different methodology. There are two main differences between them:

- The theoretical framework (see Table 3.1)
- The questionnaires and answers

In the Factors and Quality (F&Q) study (OECD 2005b) the data is drawn from PISA 2000 context questionnaires to school principals, while the *Education at a Glance* data is drawn from responses in questionnaires given to panels of experts (as discussed above).

The advantage of the F&Q study over the OECD's *Education at a Glance* study is that the questionnaire is drawn from the same sample of PISA 2000 schools. Therefore, answers are given by principals from sampled schools and presumably subject to generalization. Criticism of the F&Q study is based not on the statistical merits but on the acquisition of data and on the conclusion or claims drawn from the data set.

F&Q asks the question: "Is there a relationship between school autonomy and student performance?" (OECD 2005b, p.71). In general the wording used by the drafters of this document is very broad. However, in the end the drafters are tempted to tilt the balance towards 'the-higher-the-autonomy-the-better-the-performance' recipe as is evident from the following paragraph:

> In other words, on average, student performance in reading is higher in schools with more responsibility. More specifically, if a school's autonomy in one of the OECD countries is one standard deviation above the international average, its mean performance in reading literacy is nearly 7 score points higher than the performance of the average OECD school. Taking into account all countries, this effect is even larger. If a school's autonomy in one of the PISA countries is one standard deviation above the international average, its average performance is nearly 9 score points higher than the average PISA school. This finding suggests that decentralised education systems are more advantageous for students than centralised systems (OECD 2005b, p.71).

When the results are controlled by factors to do with students and schools, the positive relationship between quality and autonomy becomes blurred:

> The PISA 2000 results only partly support the widespread positive expectations that exist with respect to school autonomy and the internal decentralisation of decision-making. The expected results are only found when the models are unadjusted for student background and school-level characteristics (OECD 2005b, p.73).

This ambiguity is confirmed by my study. Vagueness in education and school policies such as decentralization and autonomy means that education systems around the world are not converging.

Comparison between the OECD's and this Study

The 'Education at a Glance' Study
The two studies (OECD and this one) are not directly comparable since the systems are classified according to different school levels (lower secondary schools only for the OECD's sample versus lower and upper secondary schools in this sample) and different affiliations (public or state schools only in the OECD's study versus all affiliations in my study). They also offer two different methods of measuring the devolution of power and autonomy. Furthermore, they show some of the difficulties in the analysis of ideas and concepts such as decentralization and autonomy as they are transferred, translated or imported into different cultural, political and institutional settings. For the purposes of my research, consistency in the two studies is not needed. The aim is to see if the two studies have enough information to suggest that patterns can be derived in school education policies. If different studies show a sound reasonable indication of patterns and best practices, then we may have a case for convergence.

There are few countries that are included in both samples. Table 3.2 shows the countries in the OECD's studies and the countries and regions in my study. They are listed top-down as they go from a more centralized decision-making system to one less centralized in each study.

In all columns France and Mexico appear as the most centralized systems; yet one is high-performing and the other is not. Surprisingly, New Zealand is seen by the OECD as very centralized – almost as close as Mexico and equal to the French system (column 1) from the central government point of view and very decentralized (column 2) from the central, state, regional or local levels of aggregation. New Zealand's

Table 3.2: Decentralization ranking of OECD's and Andere's samples from more centralization to less centralization

OECD's Sample				Andere's Sample		
Decentralization						
Public/State Secondary Schools only[1]		Public/State Secondary Schools only[2]		All Schools and Affiliations[3]	All Schools and Affiliations[4]	Public/State Secondary Schools only[5]
Mexico	30	France	79	France	France	France
New Zealand	25	Japan	78	Mexico	Mexico	Mexico
France	24	Mexico	77	New Zealand	New Zealand	Czech Rep.
Sweden	18	Australia	76	Czech Republic	Czech Rep.	England
Japan	13	Finland	73	Korea	United Kingdom	Finland
England	11	Sweden	54	Finland	Korea	Australia (ACT)
Korea	9	Korea	51	Japan	Australia	Sweden
Czech Rep.	7	Czech Rep.	40	United Kingdom	Finland	
Finland	2	New Zealand	25	Sweden	Japan	
Australia	0	England	15	Australia	Sweden	

Sources:
1. Ranked by percentage of decisions taken at the central level (OECD 2004b, p.431, Table D6).
2. Ranked by percentage of decisions taken at the central, state, provincial/regional, sub-regional and local levels (OECD 2004b, p.431, Table D6.1).
3. Ranked from more to less centralized at the central level of government (national or federal).
4. Ranked from more to less centralized at the state, regional, or local level of government.
5. Ranked from more to less centralized at the state, regional or local level of government and for public or state lower-secondary schools only.
Note: ACT=Australian Capital Territory.

Tomorrow's Schools reform sandwiched the system into two main stakeholders – the school and the central/national Ministry of Education. There were no intermediaries between the two – therefore, more centralization. If the analysis of the system is presented as in column 2, then New Zealand is seen as highly decentralized since most countries in this sample reported to have some sort of consultation with schools when making decisions. The comparison between the two models falls apart when looking at the level of analysis, namely lower secondary schools only in the OECD's sample (Table 3.2, column 1) and only public secondary schools in Andere's sample[5] (Table 3.2, column 5). There were no schools in Andere's sample with the lower secondary only characteristic for New Zealand as they are drawn from lower secondary schools attached to upper secondary schools. This is why

---

[5] In order to close the methodological gap of the two studies, I have reduced the size of my sample to the surveys of lower secondary public (government-run) schools only. Obviously, the number of observations is reduced drastically.

New Zealand is missing from the column 5 ranking. Lower secondary schools, as usually understood (years 7 to 9, ISCED2),[6] or the first three years after six years of primary education (ISCED1) are non-existent in New Zealand. The vast majority of lower secondary schools and their students in New Zealand are attached to upper secondary schools or form part of upper secondary schools.

The school education system in New Zealand is particularly different. Most lower-secondary students attend schools that organize schooling in lower secondary and upper secondary sections together – for example, from Grade 7 to Grade 13 secondary schools or from Grade 9 to Grade 13 secondary schools (New Zealand Ministry of Education 2005). There are different types of schools in New Zealand for primary and secondary school education (New Zealand Ministry of Education 2001). In most cases students go directly from primary schools to secondary schools with intermediate years incorporated into the secondary schools. Thus there are no lower secondary schools that fit the neat category based on ISCED of the lower secondary category and assumed by the OECD's model. This is also true in the Czech Republic, where the organization of schools is very complex and differs from the neat 6-3-3 school education system that we observe in some countries and systems around the world. Whether or not panelists from the OECD's analysis took this structural matter into account is not clear. If all schools or most schools in New Zealand are structured as lower plus upper secondary schools under the same premises, decision-making analysis cannot be compared with countries such as Mexico, France, Finland, Korea, Switzerland and Japan, where schools are clearly structurally divided between lower secondary and upper secondary. Units being compared (schools and decision-making processes or policies) are not comparable. Therefore, claiming that less centralization is better than more centralization or that more autonomy is better than less autonomy as best policies to explain students' performance such as in PISA is not correct.

There is more information that can be analyzed in both studies. The OECD's study has a variable called "percentage of decisions taken by schools in public sector lower-secondary education, by mode [full autonomy, consultation with others, within a framework and other] and domain [organization of instruction, personnel management, planning and structure of schooling and curricula and allocation and use of resources] of decision making" (OECD 2004b, pp.426-428). My analysis

---

[6] ISCED: International Standard Classification of Education.

of the autonomy of schools was first divided into three different levels: school level, the level of the principal and that of the teachers. Then it was further broken down into different levels and not only modes. The OECD's categories cannot be compared directly with this study in the autonomy variable either. The unit of analysis in OECD's study is blurred by the organization of the systems in each country or region or by the complexities of decision-making in each school or in each district. The perceptions of experts from OECD's panel do not coincide with the perceptions of experts, principals or teachers in my sample. For instance, in Table 3.3 where autonomy in schools is measured, Australia shows very little autonomy in the OECD's study compared with others, whereas in my sample Australia is fairly high in autonomy. Who is right? Well, both and neither. Again, the Australian system embraces many systems of education. Whether the panelists from the OECD's study were talking about the system as a whole or that of New South Wales or any other of the seven states is difficult to know. In this study only one of the eight schools visited belonged to the lower secondary level and it is located in the Australian Capital Territory (ACT), in itself a district with a very high academic record for school education. Does this reflect the reality of Australia? Not at all. Australia is a complex, territorially decentralized school education system where different political and institutional realities define relations between schools and local authorities. The analysis is again lost in a sea of complexities of systems.

The opening paragraph of Chapter D of the OECD's *Education at a Glance* 2004 (OECD 2004b, p.423) states:

> Overall, decisions are most highly centralised (taken at the central and/or state level of government) in Australia, Austria, Greece, Luxembourg, Mexico, Portugal, Spain and Turkey, with central government particularly dominant in Greece (88% of decisions taken by the central administration) and Luxembourg (66%).

Looking back at Table 3.2, column 1, Australia is ranked (by the OECD study) as the most decentralized of all countries if we measure decentralization at the level of central government – an OECD definition. And yet, the above paragraph offers a conclusion that contrasts sharply with the observation in Table 3.2. The OECD's decision to present data as central plus state level of government decision-making changes the story completely. Should we then call the Australian school system centralized or decentralized? Should we then say that, since Australia is a high-performing country, centralization of decision-making is good or bad? It makes no sense to talk about these factors in a comparative way. We cannot say anything more without falling into a world of ambiguities. To make sense of this we need to enter the in-depth case-narrative analysis of the intricacies, characteristics, histories and stories of decision-making and autonomy in each school education system. Let's look at more examples related to autonomy of schools.

Table 3.3: Autonomy ranking of OECD's sample and Andere's sample from more autonomy to less autonomy (full autonomy, consultation and framework*)

OECD's Sample				Andere's Sample	
Autonomy					
Public/State Secondary Schools only[1]		Public/State Secondary Schools only[2]		All Schools of All Affiliations[3]	Public/State Secondary Schools only[4]
New Zealand	45	England	85	New Zealand	England
Sweden	43	New Zealand	75	Sweden	Australia (ACT)
England	42	Czech Rep.	60	Australia	Sweden
Korea	29	Korea	48	England	Finland
Finland	23	Sweden	47	Japan	Mexico
France	21	France	32	Finland	Czech Rep.
Mexico	13	Finland	27	Mexico	France
Australia.	9	Australia	24	Korea	
Japan	9	Japan	23	Czech Rep.	
Czech Rep.	6	Mexico	23	France	

Sources:
1.   Ranked by percentage of decisions taken at the school level in full autonomy (OECD 2004, p.434, Table D6.3).
2.   Ranked by percentage of decisions taken at the school level in full autonomy and within a framework, and other (OECD 2004, p.434, Table D6.3).
3.   Ranked from more to less autonomy as perceived by interviewees of all schools of all affiliations, all things considered.
4   Ranked from more to less autonomy as perceived by interviewees of public/state lower-secondary interviewees only, all things considered.
Note: ACT=Australian Capital Territory
* OECD's definition of autonomy (decision-making) by mode (OECD 2004b, p.431).

Table 3.3 and 3.4 refer to autonomy of schools that are very similar but with minor changes. Table 3.3 defines autonomy, 'all things considered' and all modes (OECD). Table 3.4 defines autonomy, 'all things considered' and all modes and domains considered (OECD). The results in ranking are very similar, with changes only in column 2 of Table 3.4 as compared with Table 3.3.

Table 3.4: Autonomy rank of decision-making in OECD's sample and overall autonomy in Andere's sample, from more autonomy to less autonomy by mode* (full autonomy, consultation, framework and other) and domain* (organization of instruction, personnel management, planning and structures, resources)

OECD's Sample		Andere's Sample		
Autonomy				
Public/State Secondary Schools only[1]		Public/State Secondary Schools only[2]		All Schools of All Affiliations[3]	Public/State Secondary Schools only[4]
New Zealand	45.75	New Zealand	85.50	New Zealand	England
Sweden	42.75	England	85.00	Sweden	Australia (ACT)
England	42.25	Czech Rep.	60.50	Australia	Sweden
Korea	29.25	Korea	48.00	England	Finland
Finland	23.00	Finland	43.75	Japan	Mexico
France	20.75	Sweden	40.75	Finland	Czech Rep.
Mexico	12.50	France	35.50	Mexico	France
Australia	9.50	Japan	28.50	Korea	
Japan	9.50	Australia	24.50	Czech Rep.	
Czech Rep.	6.50	Mexico	22.25	France	

Sources:
1. Ranked by percentage of decisions taken at the school level in full autonomy by domain of decision-making (OECD 2004, p.435, Table D6.4). In calculating the percentages, data was drawn from OECD's Table D6.4, and only as it relates to the 'full autonomy' percentages for the four domains (organization of instruction, personnel management, planning and structures and resources): The four domain values were added, each with a 25% weighting.
2. Ranked by percentage of decisions taken at the school level in consultation, within a framework or other by domain of decision-making (OECD 2004, p.435, Table D6.4). In calculating the percentages, data was drawn from OECD's Table D6.4, and only as it relates to 'consultation, within a framework or other' criteria for four domains (organization of instruction, personnel management, planning and structures and resources). The four values were added, each with a 25% weighting.
3. Ranked from more to less autonomy, as perceived by interviewees of all schools of all affiliations, all things considered.
4. Ranked from more to less autonomy, as perceived by interviewees of public/state lower secondary interviewees only, all things considered.
Note: ACT=Australian Capital Territory.
* OECD's definitions of autonomy (decision-making) by domain and mode (OECD 2004b, p.431).

We could start talking about autonomy in a broad sense, all things considered (Tables 3.3 and 3.4), to narrow the focus later under specific domains or criteria (Table 3.5). Table 3.4 shows consistency across everything for New Zealand in the OECD's and my samples (since schools in New Zealand are autonomous in all respects), but not for countries such as Australia or Korea or Japan, where the comparative analysis loses ground because the level of analysis (of the school systems) differs from one country to the next. For example, since this sample was based on PISA-type schools (fifteen-year-olds), almost all the sampled students for PISA in Australia, Japan and Korea are students enrolled in upper secondary schools. This explains why Japan and Korea do not appear in column 4 of Table 3.4.

Looking at these results one wonders why the OECD's publication, *Economic Survey of Mexico,* cited above (OECD 2005, p.54), and Guichard's (2005, p.16), talk about benchmarks or OECD's best practices (OECD 2005, p.10) if the evidence seems to show that there are no best practices in school autonomy.

Let us then look in more detail at the meaning of autonomy. Autonomy is a difficult concept to measure, which is why the OECD and I both divided the concept into domains (OECD) or criteria, which was the approach taken by me. One of the most important areas to test autonomy in schools is the organization of instruction in the OECD's framework or curriculum in the criteria of this study. Table 3.5 shows the OECD's results as opposed to my results, but only as they relate to the question of autonomy in curriculum.

Table 3.5: Autonomy ranking from more autonomy to less autonomy by mode* (full autonomy, consultation, framework and other) and domain* (organization of instruction in OECD's samples and curriculum in Andere's sample) of decision-making

OECD's Sample				Andere's Sample	
Autonomy					
Public/State Secondary Schools only[1]		Public/State Secondary Schools only[2]		All Schools of All Affiliations[3]	Public/State Secondary Schools only[4]
New Zealand	88	New Zealand	100	Japan	Australia (ACT)
England	75	England	100	Sweden	Sweden
Finland	75	Australia	88	Australia	Finland
France	75	Czech Rep.	88	Finland	Czech Rep.
Korea	75	Finland	88	Korea	Mexico
Sweden	75	France	75	New Zealand	England
Mexico	50	Korea	75	Czech Rep.	France
Australia	38	Mexico	75	England	
Japan	38	Japan	63	Mexico	
Czech Rep.	13	Mexico	63	France	

Sources:
1. Ranked by percentage of decisions taken at the school level in full autonomy by domain of decision-making (OECD 2004, p.435, Table D6.4). In calculating the percentages, data was drawn from OECD's Table D6.4, and only as it relates to the 'In full autonomy' percentages for one domain only, namely 'organization of instruction.'
2. Ranked by percentage of decisions taken at the school level in consultation, within a framework or other by domain of decision-making (OECD 2004, p.435, Table D6.4). In calculating the percentages, data was drawn from OECD's Table D6.4, and only as it relates to 'Consultation, within a framework or other' criteria in one domain only, namely 'organization of instruction.'

3.   Ranked from more to less autonomy as perceived by interviewees of all schools, all affiliations, as per the criteria of school curricula or curriculum.
4.   Ranked from more to less autonomy as perceived by interviewees of public/state lower secondary interviewees only according to the criteria of school curricula or curriculum.

Table 3.5 shows the results from the two studies in four columns in the domain (OECD) of "organization of instruction" and the criteria of curriculum as two close concepts. The rankings of the two models show similarities but also differences. OECD's column 1 ranks New Zealand as the country with highest autonomy in "organization of instruction" over countries such as England, Finland, Australia and Korea. In column 3, I have New Zealand ranked below all these countries. Why is this so? In the first place, my ranking in column 3 has ranked countries for a sample that includes all types of schools with 15-year-old students. As already seen, New Zealand's education system does *not* allow us to make a neat 6-3-3 distribution of education levels. Given this fact, one could ask again why the panels of experts in the OECD's analysis were making judgments about the autonomy of a lower secondary school that does not exist in theory or in practice. The distinction is not trivial. Lower secondary schools tend to show different organizational, managerial and resource operations than upper secondary schools or lower secondary schools attached to primary schools.

The considerable variety in all countries represented in my study shows the great difficulty in defining concepts such as decentralization and autonomy. Even after long discussions to secure a common under-standing about the scope of each question in the survey, principals and teachers and experts from each educational background gave different weights and different answers to the same question. What is important is that, taking all answers from all people in all countries together, they do not show convergence. Decentralization and autonomy are concepts rather too ambiguous to define.

The Factors and Quality Study
Since my study is based on questionnaires to PISA-type schools, it should be more comparable with the OECD's F&Q study. However, as is shown below, and judging from the findings of the two studies, similarities are found only in a few cases.

One of the sources of the differences between the F&Q and this study is that the former is based only on questionnaires to principals in a small section of a long context questionnaire; the latter, however, is based on a long questionnaire and interviews. In my study, before the question was answered by the principal, some exchange of ideas and concepts occurred between the interviewee and the researcher. These exchanges were made with the purpose of securing homogeneity in meaning.

The sample of comparable countries in both studies is larger and more consistent in all areas of inquiry, as is shown in the following tables. I draw only on a few examples to show the similarities and differences in the two studies.

Let us compare the two studies under the domain of "Curriculum and Instruction." There are few similarities. Let us take three of the four cases discussed in Chapter 2 – New Zealand, Mexico and the US. These cases demonstrate wide differences in the two studies as seen in Table 3.6. New Zealand is at the top in my study, reflecting the fact that interviewees see the schools (as an entity) to be very autonomous. The highest authority of schools in New Zealand is the school board. Therefore, seeing the school as an autonomous entity is like saying that the school board has a great deal of responsibility, as implied in the OECD's F&Q study. By almost all measures, schools in New Zealand are seen as autonomous; they are certainly more autonomous than most of the countries listed above New Zealand in the OECD's columns in

Table 3.6: The OECD's Curriculum and Instruction Domain and Andere's Curriculum Domain at the School Level

OECD's Curriculum Domain[1]	Students enrolled in schools with autonomy (%)	Andere's Curriculum[2]
Hong Kong	41.2	New Zealand
United States	40.2	Ireland
Chile	35.5	Sweden
Canada	13.4	Australia
Belgium	12.4	Finland
OECD	12.1	UK
Ireland	10.4	Hong Kong
Mexico	9.3	Belgium
Switzerland	9.0	Rest of the World (RW)
Finland	8.7	Czech Republic
Czech Republic	8.1	Chile
New Zealand	7.0	United States
Australia	6.6	Korea
United Kingdom	5.4	Japan
Korea	2.2	Canada
Sweden	1.6	Switzerland
Japan	0.5	Mexico

Sources:
1. Ranked from more to less autonomy according to the percentages of students enrolled in schools where principals report that the school board has some responsibility for curriculum and instruction (OECD 2005b, p.136, Table 5.5).
2. Ranked from more to less autonomy based on an ordinal comparison of median values of perceptions.

Table 3.6. Mexico is listed as more autonomous than New Zealand, whereas in this study Mexico is at the bottom of the ranking table next to Switzerland, which I believe more accurately reflects reality. Even though the United States is known as one of the most decentralized school systems in the world, schools may not be as autonomous as schools in New Zealand. One of the reasons for this is that schools in the US have a strong relationship with an outside district school board.

Why is it that if the two studies are based (in theory) on PISA schools (OECD's F&Q study) or PISA-type schools (my study) they show such differences in findings – at least at the school level? One reason might be that the questionnaires in the F&Q study are not searching enough to test reality. Reviewing the questions of the F&Q study and the possible answer, it is easy to see how principals might be confused.

In the F&Q study principals were given a questionnaire with 22 main questions. Question 22 is divided into 12 sub-questions from a) to l) with five possible boxes (1 to 5) for principals to tick:

'In your school, who has the main responsibility for: (Please <tick> as many boxes as appropriate in each row.)'
1) Not a school responsibility
2) Appointed or elected board
3) Principal
4) Department head
5) Teachers

The 12 sub-questions:
a) Hiring teachers
b) Firing teachers
c) Establishing teachers' starting salaries
d) Determining teachers' salary increases
e) Formulating the school budget
f) Deciding on budget allocations within the school
g) Establishing student disciplinary policies
h) Establishing student assessment policies
i) Approving students for admittance to school
j) Choosing which textbooks are used
k) Determining course content
l) Deciding which courses are offered

From the questionnaire framework, the OECD's drafting experts drew some models and correlations that I think lacked information. Allow me to explain. If I were a principal and saw a questionnaire like this, I might well tick more boxes because all possible answers are true, or I might tick none since there might be the case that principals perceive no clear autonomy in each question or all questions. There is no way to confirm that principals answered consistently across the board. Some may have chosen to tick many boxes and others fewer boxes. The source of the uncertainty for principals is that there are schools around the world that do not have school boards but governing bodies (like external school boards, the local government, the church, the district school board). How then do we know how principals answered this question? For other schools, school boards inside the school are advisory boards, involved but with no decision-making authority. How do we know that principals were consistent when answering the question on advisory boards as opposed to decision-making boards? In some schools, principals who sit on school boards have a voice but no vote, while in others the principal has a voice and a vote. How then do we know how the principals understood and answered the questions since in both cases the board and the principal are intertwined?

Let us take the questions as they relate to the principals. Some schools have very strong principals with strong personalities and styles, where the principal's control of things is not in question. Yet in other schools, typically in German cantons in Switzerland, schools are run without principals. How do we know that principals, or whoever answered the questionnaires, were consistent about the role of principals in all 12 questions? There is no way of knowing except via an interview.

Take the issue of department heads and teachers. There are many schools around the world, especially small schools, that do not have the luxury of department heads, but teachers still attempt to select textbooks in consultation with the principal or vice-principal or among a group of other teachers. How the principal construes the questions in such circumstances is very difficult to know. And since the department heads are also teachers, how do we know whether, in ticking the answers, they consistently answered only one of the boxes or the two boxes. Some probably ticked one and some both, reflecting the same situation. If they did not answer in a consistent way, then the numbers in percentages reported by the OECD may mislead us instead of guiding us, as I think happened in Table 3.6, with the case of New Zealand, the US and Mexico.

Let us look at one more example. Table 3.7 shows the findings of the two studies for the financial resources domain.
New Zealand springs to mind, given the extreme difference. The first observation is that principals do not run schools like businesses. They do not have a budget as in the business sense, an annual budget that includes everything that the principal can handle and financially manage. Thus, talk of financial autonomy in schools has to be taken to the level of schools where there might also be very little maneuverability. In this sense schools around the world share the same picture. Within the small fraction of money at their disposal and all the budgetary rules,

principals are free to move around, with exception. In Mexico, for instance, principals cannot have more autonomy than (or similar to) principals in New Zealand as the column for the OECD's F&Q study in Table 3.7 shows. Principals in Mexico do not even have a budget within which to operate. The difference in the two systems is shown by the column on the right in Table 3.7. So, it is difficult to see how principals in Mexico understood the OECD's questions. Furthermore, principals in New Zealand are important actors and they are very highly paid. The reform drafters in the 1980s in New Zealand saw the position of principal in the schools as key to the success of the Tomorrow's Schools initiative. Internal school boards in New Zealand are very powerful and autonomous, but that does not mean that principals aren't. How the principals and boards relate in the power-structure interaction is something that has to be studied case-by-case at the school level.

Table3.7: The OECD's Financial Resources Domain and Andere's Management of Budget at the Principal Level

OECD's Financial Resources Domain[1]	Students enrolled in schools with autonomy (%)	Andere's Management of Budget[2]
Sweden	79.9	New Zealand
Czech Republic	74.5	Sweden
Korea	68.4	Australia
Australia	66.3	United Kingdom
Finland	62.1	Ireland
Canada	56.7	Korea
Japan	52.0	Hong Kong
OECD	48.9	United States
Belgium	48.8	Rest of the World (RW)
Ireland	46.5	Canada
Hong Kong	45.7	Belgium
United States	43.1	Chile
Mexico	40.9	Japan
New Zealand	38.7	Finland
United Kingdom	35.9	Czech Republic
Switzerland	25.7	Switzerland
Chile	21.0	Mexico

Sources:
1. Ranked from more to less autonomy according to the percentages of students enrolled in schools where principals report that the principal has some responsibility for financial resources (OECD 2005b, p.134 Table 5.3).
2. Ranked from more to less autonomy based on an ordinal comparison of median values of perceptions.

Findings on Decentralization, Autonomy and Quality

Does more decentralization and/or autonomy in schools mean more quality in education outcomes? Do students who come from decentralized systems of education perform consistently higher in international assessments?

Experts within the OECD and the World Bank seem to believe that more decentralization and more autonomy are better, regardless of the context, location, situation or history of school education systems. Take for instance the much-cited paragraphs in this chapter about best practices (OECD 2005a, p.54; Guichard 2005, p.16). Or consider the F&Q study, (OECD 2005b), as seen above. Or consider the following paragraph from *Education at a Glance*:

> Various motives are attributed to the desire to increase the autonomy of schools, such as enhancing the quality, effectiveness and responsiveness of schooling (OECD 2004b, p.424).

One special issue of the International Journal of Educational Development in 1996 was "devoted to a critical examination of [The World Bank's] *Priorities and Strategies for Education*" (Watson 1996, p.213; original italics, my parenthesis). In the editorial, Watson says, "These strategies [the World Bank's] are offered to educational policy makers in developing countries if they wish to receive funding from the bank. Since the Bank accounts for 25% of all bilateral and multilateral assistance to education this is an important source of influence" (Watson 1996, p.213; my parenthesis). One of the strategies cited by Watson (1996, p.213) represents "more emphasis on institutional autonomy."

Does the data from the two studies support the relationship between decentralization/autonomy and performance?

Countries depicted in Tables 3.2 to 3.7 are high-performing countries since all of them, except for Mexico, performed well above the OECD's mean score in both PISA 2000 and PISA 2003. And yet in all shown classifications there are countries that seem to be more decentralized than others and more autonomous than others. For instance, at the country level Table 3.2 column 1 (OECD's sample) shows high-performing countries such as New Zealand and Finland at opposite ends of the centralization–decentralization scale; column 2 shows Japan and New Zealand, two high-performing countries, as opposites too. If we go to columns 3, 4 and 5 (my sample) from the same table we see much the same discrepancies.

Much the same seems to apply to the autonomy of schools side of the story. See Table 3.3. Column 1 (the OECD's study) shows high-performing countries New Zealand and Sweden at the top of the autonomy scale and high-performing countries Japan and the Czech Republic at the bottom, and Finland in the middle. Column 3 tells a similar story, with New Zealand and Sweden at the top and the Czech Republic and France at the bottom.

Let us finally take the issue of autonomy in schools from the "organization of instruction" (OECD) or "curriculum" – the point of view taken by this study. This is shown in Table 3.5. Column 1 shows New Zealand and England very high in the autonomy and Japan and the Czech Republic very low. Again, all of them are high-performers. Column 3 shows Japan as very high and the Czech Republic and England as low in autonomy, with France as the lowest of this reduced list, and again all of them high-performers.

There are too few countries in these two samples in Tables 3.2 to 3.7 to tell scientifically sound stories of a relationship between performance and decentralization or autonomy as it is claimed for some factors by the OECD (OECD 2005b).

Countries may import policies and practices, but when those finally arrive in districts and schools they are subjected to the translation, implementation and sense-making filters. Each filtering layer will reshape the traveling, imported or transferred policies and practices according to the history of schooling, the resources available and the political and human networks at hand. One school principal from a very high-performing country put it bluntly in one of the interviews, "Of course, they [the local or national authorities] will try to impose or force their decisions upon my school; however, I will only take my charge (sic) on those matters that I think are doable, right and appropriate." Another principal told me, "No, I do not follow strict instructions from above: We [teachers and I] do what we think is best for the school."

Giving due respect to the OECD's view of the world of education, there is a change in the wording in OECD's claims from 1998 to 2004 that shows a shift or recognition that stories about decentralization and autonomy are not as clear today as once believed. In 1998 the OECD's wording was:

> Concentrating decision-making close to the actual process of schooling is a strong indication of decentralisation. In 13 out of 22 OECD countries a majority of types of decisions that bear on lower secondary education are taken locally or by the school itself. (OECD 1998, p.292)

And in 2004 the OECD's remarks were:

> In 14 out of 25 countries, most types of decisions that bear on lower secondary education are taken locally or by the school itself. (OECD 2004b, p.424)

4

Autonomy, Assessments and Accountability

I present additional findings from my study in specific areas of autonomy. Since school autonomy is a rather broad concept, the scope of the focus has been relatively narrowed to a definition of autonomy not only at the level of decision (schools, principals or teachers) but also in the areas of decision: 1) school: overall autonomy, curriculum, textbooks, school materials, timetabling, exams; 2) principals: overall autonomy, hire and removal of teachers, curriculum, timetabling, assessment of teachers, assessment of students, innovation, management and budget; 3) teachers: overall autonomy, meeting parents, curriculum, course schedule, assessing students, textbooks, innovation. The findings reported here touch upon curriculum, timetabling, management and budget, hiring and removal of teachers, as well as some traits of education systems as they relate to assessment and accountability and league tables.

The Curriculum

School curricula and timetables are key topics in every school. Figure 4.1 [1] draws, in graphical terms, the answers of all respondents to the question how autonomous are schools when making decisions related to school curriculum? This graph shows sharp variations in the answers from almost all countries. The graph shows a steep stair shape suggesting different degrees of perceived autonomy.

Figure 4.1: How autonomous are public or private schools, like your school, when making school decisions? (School curriculum)

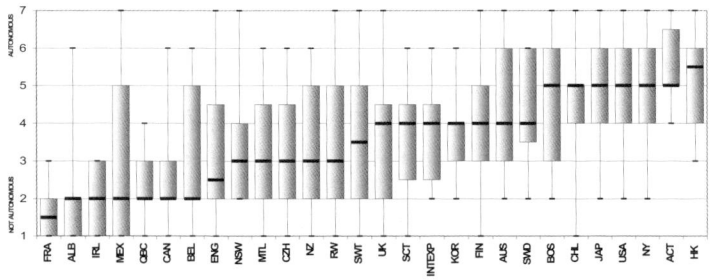

---

[1] Refer to the "How to read the graphs" section in the Introduction.

There were high-performing countries and regions in PISA 2000 or 2003 such as Hong Kong and the Australian Capital Territory (ACT) that perform at a very high level, and cities like New York (NY) and Boston (US) that do not perform very highly, and countries like Chile, that performs at a very low level – and all of them are found in the highly autonomous side of the continuum. In contrast, there are regions or countries that perform at a very high level, such as Alberta (Canada) and Flanders (Belgium), and countries that do not perform as highly, such as France, or perform at a very low level, such as Mexico – and all are located within the very low autonomy side of the spectrum. Still others, such as New Zealand, the UK, Korea and Finland, with a high-performing record, are located towards the center of the graph.

This graph has to be construed under the assumption that none of the high-performing countries, together with Mexico and Chile, has a system that allows total freedom in school education curriculum. It seems reasonable to state that, based on this data, there is convergence in the lack of autonomy in curriculum-setting, but one cannot say much more than that. Furthermore, there is no school in the high-performing countries, as per my sample, that operates its own curriculum (neither do Mexico and Chile). Even during the interviews in the prestigious private independent English schools, principals reported some duty towards the state curriculum since they are subject to governmental inspections. In Flanders, the interviewed national authorities believed they had a rather flexible, goal-oriented curriculum. However, when the same question was asked of principals and teachers, they saw the goals as too detailed and too narrow. Principals and teachers in general qualified the system with less autonomy than government experts did.

Sometimes curricula are not detailed, but framed by national examinations. Curriculum is not an easy subject to define or measure. Some of my interviewees replied to the question with the following comment: "When national examinations are strong, exams are substitutes for detailed curricula. In other words, exams define curricula as they are actually taught in schools. In these cases teachers teach to the test."

The lack of relationship between autonomy and school performance might be explained also by the example from Edmonton, Canada – a public schools district widely known and praised (Ouchi & Segal 2003) for site-based management among other things. The Edmonton Public School System (EPS) is divided into two sub-systems – known as Edmonton Public (the largest) and Edmonton Catholic. Edmonton is also well known for the high performance of its students. In PISA 2003, students from Alberta performed very highly in mathematics – as high as Hong Kong and Finland, and much higher than Canada as a whole

(Bussière et al 2004, Table B1.1, p.70). Edmonton is the second largest school district in Alberta[2] (Alberta Education 2006). However, except in a few cases, the surveyed pool of people see the schools in Alberta as having very low autonomy. The participants from this region responded to "How autonomous are public or private schools, like your school, when making decisions? (Overall)" with a median value of 4 (on a 1 to 7 scale). This answer is in line with many countries.

The rest of the answers (in topics such as curriculum, textbooks, tests, teachers' involvement in course curriculum, teachers selecting textbooks and principals' involvement in curriculum) for Edmonton gave a 'low to very low' autonomy mark in relation to the rest of the regions or countries. There are some areas, though very few, where the contrary was true: Edmonton ranks higher in autonomy than the rest of the regions or countries especially in terms of principals' ability to 'hire/ remove teachers' or evaluate/assess teachers or manage the school budget.

One principal from an EPS told me, referring to the Edmonton Catholic District: "Performance-wise the two districts (public and separate or Catholic) are very close. As a whole the Edmonton school district is based on site management or site-based decision making. In terms of school operation the primary role of principals in the Catholic system is to supervise the instruction. However, in the public system it is to run a business. We, the principals in Edmonton's public district, manage the entire thing."

Even here, as we saw before with the curriculum issue, the principals or the schools do not really manage everything. However, two different school administrations within the same city, each with different school district philosophies and operations, perform at a very high level. From this specific case we may derive convergence in performance but not in administration or education or school policies and practices.

It is not clear that principals, even in 'vanguard' market-oriented school administrations, can run schools like businesses. In the first place, in few schools in the world do principals have the authority to fire teachers or staff. In areas such as in Finland, New Zealand or Sweden, where they do have this authority, they use it very rarely. One principal in Finland explained, "I have the authority to fire permanent teachers, but I have never used it in my more than 15 years' tenure as principal."

Timetabling
One area where principals, in many cases in consensus with the teachers,

---

[2]   Alberta has two very large districts, Calgary and Edmonton, and many smaller ones. Each district can have many authorities.

can 'modify' the wishes of local or national authorities is timetabling. All curricula in the 19 (including Singapore, Chile and Mexico) countries I visited operate either under very specific detailed instructions or within a framework.

The expression 'within the framework' is widely used. The meaning of the expression is not really clear. In the English system, for example, curriculum may have a flexible framework. However, a network of national exams restricts the actual curriculum taught in schools to the topics and questions of the exams. Frameworks tend to define the core subjects, the number of sessions per week or school year, the expected outcomes per topic, the number of credits required to complete the school program successfully and the number of school days per year. Within this framework principals and teachers implement or adapt the authorities' wishes to the situation of the school. The situation of the school is defined by the following idea, as one principal from Finland told me, ". . . what is good for the children, given our own pedagogical experience (principal plus teachers) and the availability of resources – I put energy only into those things that I, along with my teachers, deem correct and appropriate."

This "I put energy" may also apply inside the classroom between teachers and students. In the 165 schools I visited and the many classrooms from each school (except perhaps for the case of Mexico), classrooms look alike, but are by no means similar. Each classroom has a different character. The same applies to schools. In most cases, although not in all, just standing outside the school before walking in, I could tell that I was in front of a school building. However, as soon as I entered the school, everything was different – from the architecture to the colors, from the ethos to the design, or from the classrooms to the size of the school. It was like entering different cultures. Take the analogy of the difference between a house and a home: houses may look alike but homes are by definition different. To paraphrase the principal from Finland, the situation of the school means that principals and teachers will respond in relation to their own experiences, expectations and networks of relationships given by the history and networks and human relationships within the school and with its stakeholders.

The micro-management of timetables may affect the macro idea of a national curriculum. When shaping the timetables, principals can reduce the number of children per classroom session by hiring more teachers or save money by increasing the number of students per classroom and therefore hiring fewer teachers. Saving money can increase information and telecommunication technologies in the school, but it can also increase guidance, staff development or clean and hygienic ablution facilities. In almost all high-performing countries principals make these decisions whether they have a school board within the school or not. When shaping timetables principals can shorten or lengthen the school day, allowing students to go home earlier or later. Timetables may increase the number of hours devoted to remedial classes or to after-school day counseling. Timetables may be distributed during the calendar year in one section or several sections, allowing principals and teachers to schedule timetables in a sequential order and in a flexible way so that students can tailor their own program. There are schools in New Zealand, Canada, Finland and the US with flexible timetables so that, with some guidance, students can write their own programs at their own pace. Students can also follow a more traditional timetable in the same school. Students can accelerate their pace or slow it down according to their choice and the opportunities the school offers. Schools and students in Ireland can decide on an optional transition year after lower or junior secondary graduation. In the transition year schools are able to run their own curriculum.

In one mathematics class in New Zealand students from all levels of upper secondary education (Years 10, 11 and 12) were taking the same Year 11 level to suit their own pace of learning. Yet in Edmonton, in a very large classroom the size of a tennis court, students were conducting their own studies, with several teachers dealing with questions on a one-to-one basis. Principals can also arrange timetables so that all mathematics or science or English courses are either squeezed into a few weeks or spread over many weeks. In practice, principals and teachers not only make their own sense of policies dictated or induced from national or local authorities; they also fine-tune such policies and regulations according to their wishes inside the school and classrooms. What happens inside the school and the classroom can affect the curriculum.

The Management of Budgets and Hiring and Removing Teachers
Principals, in most cases, do not have a real budget to operate within schools and even when they do, they are constrained by many regulatory bodies. These include those inside the school (school boards) and outside (district school boards, regulations, inspections and/or supervision). The bulk of a school's budget is made up of the salaries (plus fringe benefits) of teachers and personnel. Some principals have some room to maneuver school budgets, but they receive very little cash and have minimal control over salaries and benefits. In many cases principals receive no cash, but a bookkeeping account of their cash managed by others (usually local authorities).

The lack of a budget or budget control is another indication of the limited power schools have in managing human resources and schools as business entities. The finding here is that principals do not have the autonomy to manage schools along business lines. However, they do find ways to manage the schools along pedagogical lines. The marketization movement has reached schools only in rhetoric. One additional limitation is human resources' management. Teachers everywhere are still very powerful. And I do not mean only teachers' unions.

Figure 4.2: How autonomous are principals of public or private schools, like your school, when making decisions? (Hiring/removing teachers)

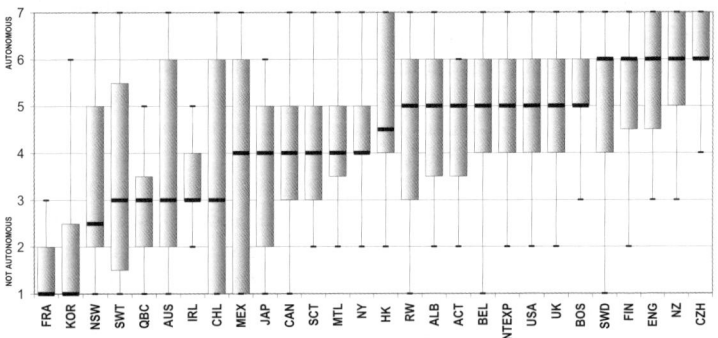

Figure 4.2 seems to indicate that principals generally have (see the median value of five for the RW—rest of the world—observation) a fairly large capacity to hire and remove teachers, though a deeper inquiry revealed a contrary picture. The graph, however, illustrates the freedom of hiring rather than the freedom of removing teachers. In time, and too late to make the changes, I realized that the two decisions cannot be merged into a single question. If the question had been divided into two parts, namely one for hiring and one for firing, the answers I would have obtained would have been the same or similar for hiring but different for firing. Principals seldom fire teachers or staff, just as school boards (inside or outside schools) seldom fire principals. Even when principals do have the authority to fire teachers, they rarely use it since in practice there are many potential 'legal' costs when firing a teacher.

Teachers in turn can make the life of principals even more difficult. Surprisingly, teachers can affect principals' abilities to manage human resources, whether they act alone or collectively. Permanent teachers know that their immovability can limit the principal's plan for change, innovation or motivation. They are able to mobilize other teachers against the principal. Eventually, this has the potential for irate interactions between the principal and the teacher(s). In my sample there were schools where teachers were able to dominate the principal's authority by blocking decisions or putting obstacles in the way of decisions for change before they could be implemented. Principals or schools from my sample, whether they are from high performing countries or not, do not really have the power to hire and fire teachers at will. The autonomy of schools and principals does not seem to be related to high performance either.

Nonetheless, schools, school districts and school education systems have learnt to circumvent the rigidity of teachers, at least temporarily. One strategy is to hire teachers under a period of probation or training, or as substitutes for absent teachers. This tactic reduces the likelihood of principals or school boards hiring teachers who are not really committed to teaching and teamwork; it also postpones the main hiring decision for a year or two. When the teachers are finally hired in permanent positions, the possibility of personnel management challenges arise. However, in all cases principals only spoke about difficulties with personnel management in exceptional cases. In general schools find ways to perform highly despite labor limitations.

There are other ways to solve this problem of rigidity of teachers. One of these is the rotation-of-teachers policy followed in Korea, though not all principals think this is a good idea. In districts such as Edmonton, principals cannot really fire a teacher, but may ask the superintendent's office to transfer teachers they wish to 'remove.' In Mexico principals and supervisors may negotiate with local authorities and the union to transfer a teacher from one school into an administrative position in the offices of the local authority or the union.

The general rule in high-performing countries, then, is that principals can hire or have a say in hiring teachers. However, they can very rarely fire them. Some schools still seem to be able to perform highly against impossible odds and the teachers' inability to accept change is not seen as a hurdle to quality. Why is this so? In a business-like organization labor mobility and flexibility are seen as absolutely fundamental to the company's success in a competitive environment.

One possible answer is that this rigidity of view is coupled with high certification requirement to enter the field of teaching. In highest-performing countries where the teaching profession is highly regarded, as are the requirements to become a teacher, the quality of teachers is deemed very important. This is especially true in countries such as Finland where teachers, with relatively low salaries, are highly motivated and valued (and socially esteemed) by society at large. One way of measuring this popularity is to look at the high demand for teacher training at the universities. Teachers in Finland are often mentioned as one of the reasons for the success of Finland in PISA, despite the labor rigidity.

When my interviewees from around the globe responded with something like "teachers matter," I would reply, "Isn't that obvious?" The real question, from the systemic point of view, is what it takes to have such a qualified band of teachers. Are good teachers a function of culture? Are good teachers a function of systemic rules and practices? Finnish people like to believe that it is both culture and system or policies. However, this answer is not very helpful for policy-makers as issues of culture and history are amorphous. There is culture and history, as stated by Simola (2005), or culture and students, as stated by Jouni Välijärvi et al. (2002, p.15), in students' own "attitudes and abilities, notably engagement in reading . . . and interest in reading . . . cultural communications between parents and children." Then again, Jari Lavonen (2006) and Rasku-Puttonen[3] ascribe success to policies such as the teacher training[4] designed and implemented in 1970 or, as Raimo Vourinen[5] describes, practices such as proactive career guidance in schools. There is also a holistic view of school education success in Finland as a function of the combined effect of four intertwined factors: comprehensive and good schools for all; evolutionary rather than revolutionary educational reform; strong public institutions, the rule of law and a democratic civil society in a welfare state; and, a stable political environment (Aho et al. 2006, pp.2-3).

Assessment and Accountability Policies
Policies of assessment and accountability are another area of enormous debate. I can only highlight here the variety of high-performing countries' policies towards assessment as seen in national exams as opposed to the autonomy of schools in exams. Three questions were asked of principals and teachers and some experts about the evaluation/assessment policies and practices. Answers are shown in Figures 4.3 and 4.4.

Figure 4.3 represents the answer to the question: "How autonomous are public or private schools, like your school, when making decisions (as in exams)?" Interviewees were asked to assess the overall impact of external exams over internal exams in the following way, indicating the degree of weight:

---

[3] Personal interview in her office at the University of Jyväskylä on July 13, 2006.
[4] All teachers in Finland, class teachers and subject teachers, have to complete, more or less, three years of undergraduate work and two years of graduate work.
[5] Personal interview in his office at the University of Jyväskylä on July 07, 2006.

1. External exams (such as national exams) influencing the students' promotion from one academic year to the next
2. The extent to which external national exams are taken into account for the overall assessment of students
3. The extent to which external exams bind teachers to 'teach to the test' strategies in the classrooms

With these questions framed in such a way, participants were required to think carefully about the influence of national exams on the students' own school careers and the schools' and teachers' own teaching and learning practices. Figure 4.3 shows the answers.

Figure 4.3: How autonomous are public or private schools, like your school, when making decisions? (Exams/tests)

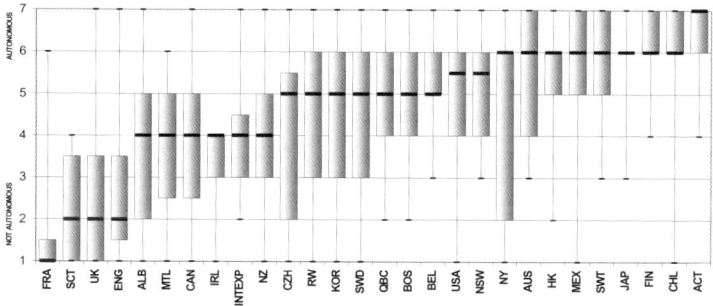

Figure 4.3 shows great variability, with a clear stepped shape indicating that countries to the left have education systems that are bound by very strong external or national assessment policies while countries to the right show considerable autonomy in the exam assessment of students regardless of the existence of national assessment policies, as in national exams. In other words, the education systems in the Australian Capital Territory, Chile, Finland, Japan, Switzerland, Mexico and Hong Kong are systems where schools' assessment policies are very strong even over national ones in determining students' promotions and the ability of schools to assess and evaluate students. In contrast, education systems in France, Scotland, and England have very strong national assessments or evaluations as in national entrance or exit exams. Interviewees or respondents were asked to consider their answers for lower secondary and upper secondary levels only. Thus countries such as Scotland which have no national exams before the end of compulsory education (around the age of fifteen or sixteen) will demonstrate a

strong influence in spite of the focus on overall school evaluations rather than national exams. Had the question focused on primary levels of education, the Scottish answers would surely have moved to the extreme right of the graph.

Note that the benchmark question for international experts[6] indicates an answer at the median level (4) with most of the answers clustered between 3 and 4.5. This means that international experts are not decided about the influence of national assessment policies on the students' own performance.

Figure 4.4 shows the answers of principals, teachers and international experts to the question: "How autonomous or independent are teachers of public or private schools, like your school, when making decisions (as self-evaluating/assessing students)?"

There is a high degree of convergence (international experts included) in this answer, showing that all surveyed people think that teachers have a say in their own students' careers, notwithstanding national exams or principals' involvement in students' evaluations school-wide. Is this convergence related to quality? Simply looking at Figure 4.4 one is tempted to answer 'Yes' to this convergence–quality question, 'but No' – after looking at the fact that Mexico and Chile (low-performing countries) have median values of 6; so the whole relationship could be blurred. However, what this seems to show is that,

Figure 4.4: How autonomous or independent are teachers of public or private schools, like your school, when making decisions? (Self-evaluating students)

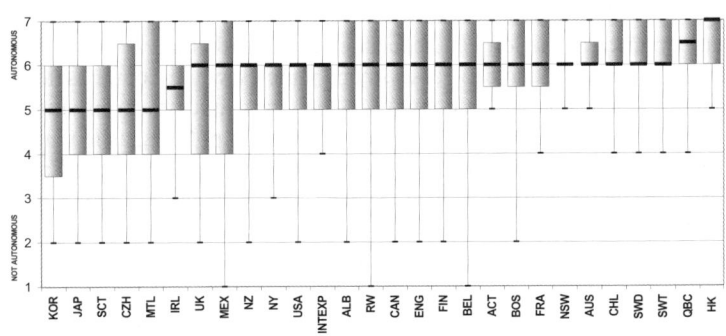

---

after years of national assessments in some countries and strong principals in others, people think that teachers remain the most important factor in students' own development.

Other than perceived knowledge, do high-performing countries have or lack national assessment policies as in national exams for the whole student population?

Finland, Flanders, the Czech Republic, New Zealand, Japan, the US, Canada and Mexico do not have national exams applied to a universal student body; there are no such exams for students in Grade 8 or Grade 9 or in areas such as mathematics, sciences, history, languages, etc. At the time of writing (2006) Mexico is moving to national exams. Countries like Finland and New Zealand maintain a dual system of random exams at lower levels and certification or 'matriculation' exams (in lieu of national exams) at upper levels. Regardless of the history of universal national examinations, all countries or systems have national assessments based on random samples. In this case they look for the overall picture rather than school-by-school, teacher-by-teacher or student-by-student assessment. Countries that have a history of universal national exams often conduct random-based testing for specific purposes. Therefore, no country in this world of high-performing countries (Mexico and Chile included) is devoid of national assessment policies, but Mexico is a relative novice in measuring and assessment. Of all the countries surveyed Mexico has the youngest school education evaluation system. Given the inexperience of Mexico in measuring and assessment of school education, one is tempted to say that convergence in assessment policies is positively related to students' performance. There are two caveats that blur such a relationship: 1) Chile, a low-performing country too, has a long history of measuring and assessment; 2) the intrinsic differences from one assessment system to the next are of paramount importance, as in the case of Scotland.

Scotland has a universal national evaluation policy for all schools, but it is done on a school-by-school basis; assessments as in exams are not compulsory and they are applied mostly at the upper secondary level or as a leaving exam for the lower or junior secondary level. Although it is a non-compulsory system, most students sit for these national exams. The rest of the grades or levels are assessed with school inspections. These inspections take detailed quantitative and qualitative indicators to guide their views and opinions. The Scottish policy is sharply different from that of their English neighbors, where universal national assessments are the order of the day with all sorts of league tables (ranking tables). Even in Ireland, school-leaving exams (especially those at the upper secondary level) are a national event, and yet league tables are banned by law. Assessment policies do not seem to be related to high performance either.

Publication of League Tables
One very sensitive issue is the publication of results or findings of assessments. How effectively are results from assessments published and how far do teachers, principals and experts agree with the publication of results in a league table format? It was difficult to find a pattern in the responses.

Figure 4.5 shows the answers to the first question: "How well are the results from assessments/evaluations (national or international) publicized in your country or region?"

The first criticism of my own inquiry was that the question should have been divided into two questions, one for international assessments and the other for national or local assessments. Even with this sub-division, answers would probably have been more skewed for national assessments (but with the same pattern). Nonetheless, there is considerable variation. Countries like Singapore, Chile, Korea, Sweden and Hong Kong report very high publication perception (6), whereas countries or regions like Flanders, DF (Mexico City), the US and New York, report very low levels. Since data from the questionnaire is not factual, errors of judgment can be expected. However, assuming that respondents were open and truthful, two things may be derived from Figure 4.5: 1) There is considerable variation in relation to publication and dissemination of assessment results; 2) the publication has not

Figure 4.5: The results of domestic and international evaluations are disseminated and publicized

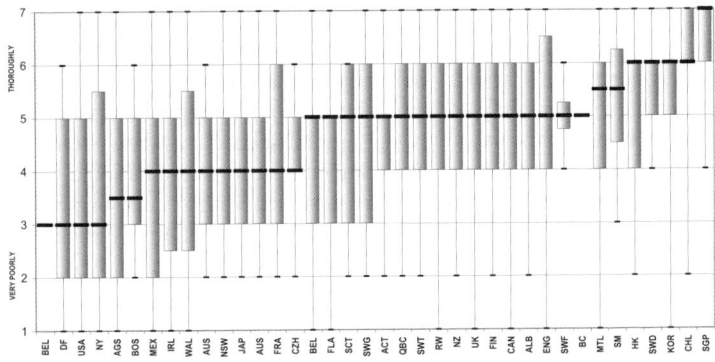

reached principals and teachers since perception is not aligned with factual evidence. If publications do not reach people, they cannot have an accountability effect. Figure 4.6 shows the answers to the question concerning agreement with the publication in a ranking or league table format.

Figure 4.6: Do you think that results of international and domestic evaluations should be made public, including the names of the schools?

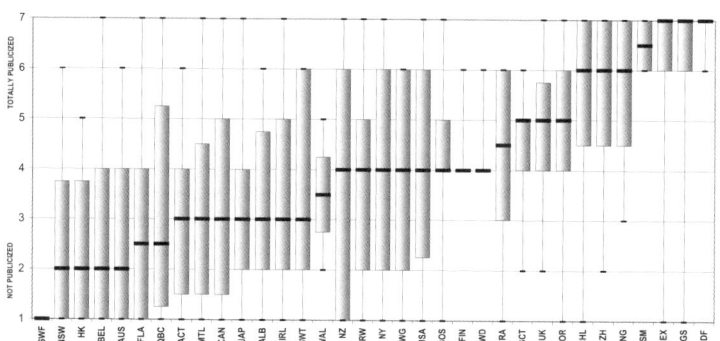

Again, the sharp stepped pattern shows a great variation in the perception of teachers, principals and experts. However, some specific comments can be made:

- Mexico is the country furthest to the right of the spectrum. Ironically, assessments of compulsory schooling in Mexico have just begun (2006) and publication of results is therefore very limited – and controlled by the state. Of all the countries in the sample, Mexico has the least history and experience in school assessments and evaluations. Not until October 2006 did the Mexican federal government publish the results of the first national assessment of primary and lower secondary education applied in the summer of 2006. My questionnaires were applied in 2004 and 2005, well before the national assessment policy was first announced.

- England, next to Mexico in the scale from 1 to 7, is the country with perhaps the most actively and openly aggressive policy towards assessments, dissemination and league tables.

- There is a cluster of high and very high-performing countries or regions (French cantons in Switzerland, New South Wales, Hong Kong, Belgium, Australia, Flanders, Quebec, Australian Capital

Territory, Montreal, Canada, Japan, Alberta, Ireland, and German cantons in Switzerland) that do not agree with open publication and, least of all, with league tables.

All in all, the issue is not decided in the minds of interviewees, and this is why the Rest of the World median sits at the neutral value of 4. Interviewees in general reacted positively when asked about the publication of results, but negatively, or at least ambiguously, when the idea of publication of league tables with names of schools was mooted. In most cases principals and teachers rejected the idea of publishing names of schools, except in places with values of 5 and above as shown in Figure 4.6. Sometimes the question evoked some discussion and debate. What worried most of my interviewees, including experts, is comparability. Are we sure that schools and systems are comparable? My interviewees showed doubts about the fairness of comparisons.

The trend seems to be that countries are publishing results with the so-called value-added methodology, with lists of schools that add value to the students as a whole, regardless of their selectivity policy or student intake (socio-economic, education and cultural or education backgrounds).

Again, in this widely debated issue that falls within the discussion of epistemic communities in areas such as comparative education, school improvement, evaluation and assessment, institutional design, competition, and accountability, the evidence seems to prove that there is no convergence. There is convergence in the application of the so-called evaluation, assessment and accountability policies among all countries and regions. There is no convergence or agreement as to the meaning of such policies or practices (much as we saw with decentralization and autonomy). The spectrum of meanings of assessment and accountability policies and practices can be so wide that one can hardly conclude that assessment policies and performance are causally related. We can not therefore borrow the policy or the idea that more assessments bring higher results.

5

Conclusions and Policy Suggestions

As the findings of this research appear to question the validity of the conclusions that can be drawn from large scale international studies, it thus raises the pertinent question of whether it is feasible for international organizations or associations to stop sponsoring or developing international studies or assessments such as TIMSS, PIRLS, PISA, SACMEQ and SERCE. I would argue that this is not the case. Comparative studies and assessments of the type conducted by IEA, OECD, SACMEQ and OREALC need to be continued, albeit with a more refined focus. Studies such as these can be very useful for measurement and inputs for diagnosis and are also useful for formative assessments for the schools that take part. However, more attention should be paid to the scope of the lessons learnt from such measurements and comparisons. Even at the comparison level, not all inputs or outputs are comparable.

Assuming reliability, which is itself a moot point, international studies of this kind are good for highlighting the differences and similarities in a given target population for some education outcomes, namely competencies, abilities and cognitive knowledge. As others before me have suggested, with different analytical or methodological tools, evidence from research such as this seems to show that conclusions from large scale studies are open to debate when explaining the causality or 'comparability' (comparing the same things) of the observed results. This confirms the complexity of the issue. Nor are these large scale studies very effective as predictive tools or recommendations for the 'transferability' of policies or practices.

The difficulties of breaking down the sample into layers (fragmentation and stratification) appear to be insurmountable if we intend to get into the complexities of school education. It seems impossible to stratify the countless characteristics of schools as belonging to the same group, in order to explain the 'whys', 'whats' and 'for whoms'. When the characteristics of one group are so different from the next, the samples need to be broken down even further so as to allow for these differences. With school and student samples gathered for the purpose of comparing not the performance of the students, but that of the schools or systems, the fragmentation should be large enough to allow for differences in the characteristics of schools and systems (context, situation, politics, history, institutions, policies, age and length of studies of sampled students).

The world of schools and schooling is complex. This complexity could be shown with the help of a ten-sided, ten-angled table (a decagon), with each column in Table 5.2, in lieu of a decagon, represented on one of the ten sides – a complex figure. The intrinsic complexity of schooling and school education policy means that making claims about best practices is a near impossible task. See, for example, Table 5.2 that shows the inherent complexity by highlighting the number of potential combinations that may occur in this limited world of 165 schools and confirms the difficulty in pin pointing individual factors. In doing comparative studies based on statistical information gathered from diverse systems, one has to make many assumptions to simplify the world. Each assumption reduces the number of possible combinations. In the process one misses the details of success stories or failures behind the schools and education systems.

The main conclusion is that international studies have a limited lending power. They can go as far as to show some differences between the sampled populations, but they cannot go around the world importing and/or exporting policies and practices at will.

To this already complex Table 5.2 we have to add more complexities such as leadership styles and personal relationships among all players but especially between principals and board members, local authorities, teachers, unions, parents and students. Besides, schools are defined by the personal histories of their students and teachers. Each student or teacher who enters a school brings with them many stories, family stories, socio-economic stories and personality stories – genes plus context or "nature and nurture."[1] In my visits to schools and during interviews with principals and teachers I was able to learn about some of these stories – both personal stories and school stories shape the everyday life of all schools in unlimited ways.

One of the complex combinations that Table 5.2 also shows is related to principals and their power relationships inside and outside the school. How do principals become principals? Where does their obligation or loyalty lie? Who are they accountable to and in which areas? How long are they expected to stay at the school as principals? Is the position of principal a reward for years of teaching? Or, is the position a merit-based job available to young or experienced teachers, school managers, policy-makers or academics?

Consider these additional but very pertinent questions: What is the parental involvement in the school at the decision-making level, advisory level, school level, classroom level, support-level, financial

---

[1] The expression is taken from David L. Kirp (2006).

level? What kinds of local authorities are related to schools: external, district, church, municipal? What kinds of school authorities are there: school boards or councils with decision-making power; advisory boards; parental and teachers' associations; student councils? How are boards composed? Are there representatives from the parents, teachers, students, alumni, government, church, business, community, village, teaching staff, and is the principal on the board? Who calls the shots on the boards? Are students directly involved in decision-making, or do they play an 'ornamental' or 'legitimizing' role?

The interaction between the different actors is a function not only of formal rules and procedures but also of personal and power relationships between them. The following questions are relevant: Who are the teachers? What is the morale of the teachers like? What is the relationship between the principal and the teachers? Are there enough resources in the school to carry out policies from local or national authorities – be they dictated, imposed or suggested? What are the ideas and preconceptions of principals and teachers? What is the relationship between the principals and the superintendent or the chief education officer from the local authority?

And answers are needed to questions like: Who are the children? What is their socio-economic background? What education do their parents have? Are parents of children currently at the school on the school board? What is the relationship between the principal and the parents?

Personal and power relationships, and their constrains, of the people who decide the policies, and the people who are supposed to implement or make sense of them, determine the final outcome, namely how policies or instructions are finally put into practice in the daily life of schools. At best, they are adapted rather than adopted.

When principals receive instructions from authorities, they react, together with some of the teachers, with questions like: Do we have the resources? Does it make sense for our children? Does this fit with our own pedagogical ideas and beliefs? Do we have the human means (teams, attitudes, motivations) from parents, teachers, children, or community, to work the policy through?

In addition to policy ideas, other concepts sometimes come to the school after traveling a long way and passing through many filters, with each filter subjected to many interpretations or translations from other players. For example, before an idea gets to the school it may have come from the international organizations to the offices of national ministers of education, then to the mid-level offices of national ministries of education; from there to state, provincial, sub-regional or local offices of education; from local or district authorities to school boards; from school boards to principals; from school principals to teachers and teaching teams; and finally to parents and children. Policies not only travel through levels but also through filters such as autocratic principals, democratic principals, decision-making boards, advisory boards, strong teachers versus weak teachers, abundant resources versus scarcity, strict rules for management of the school and resources versus flexible rules, and so on.

Furthermore, we have to add the time dimension. People and things change. Principals and teachers change – not often, but they do change. Local authorities can change too. This is rare in the case of civil servants, but frequent in the case of politicians. Children and parents in a school also change every year or at every cycle of school level. When applicable, national and state authorities also change. Regulations change, availability of financial support to schools changes and technologies change. Sometimes, by the time a researcher's observation about a school or district or education system is published, it is no longer valid since conditions in that school might have changed.

'Yes, but No'

Yes, based on international studies, we can measure and conclude that some systems, districts, schools or even students perform higher than others. We can even rank the results in league tables. But no, we cannot say why the results are the way they are, how schools or systems perform at such a high or low level, where there is consistency, what the factors of success or the obstacles that lead to failure are, or how to borrow and/or lend policies across the board. We can look at data drawn from these studies to understand better, case by case, the complexities of school education, by "contextualizing the data" (Theisen et al 1986, p.46). We can also learn that countries face similar problems and challenges: ". . . our own problems are not unique, and such knowledge can be most useful" (Noah 1986, p.155).

In an attempt to clarify the subject matter, based on the evidence this report shows, let me add to the convergence and divergence dimension of school education the dimension of comparability and transferability. It is one thing to compare and quite another to transfer. Some school education concepts are comparable, but they cannot travel or, if they do, they are not transferable. Based on a simple model of education and school policies (inputs, processes and outputs), adapted from many sources including the OECD's own model (OECD 2005b, p.12), Table 5.1 seeks to clarify the complex world of comparability and transferability for the two opposite views of a converging or diverging world of school education. This table shows the relationship between convergence and divergence and comparability and transferability of school education concepts. It shows where there is convergence and where there is divergence in school education, and whether inputs, processes, policies and practices, and outputs are comparable or transferable or both. Therefore, the school education world is converging and diverging at the same time.

Table 5.1: Convergence and Divergence; Comparability and Transferability

	Comparability		Transferability	
	Yes	No	Yes	No
	Inputs			
Convergence	Number of teachers and schools			Resources
	Textbooks		Textbooks with adaptations	
	Curriculum structures and subjects		Curriculum structures and subjects	Curriculum implementation Teaching and learning inside the classroom
	Financial commitments	Nature and level of financial commitment		Payroll policies
	Outputs			
	Measuring scores Measuring size of systems Measuring learning	Fairness of scores	Methods to measure goals and performance	Goals of education
Divergence	**Processes, Policies and Practices**			
	Rhetoric, Labels, Talking	Decentralization Autonomy Assessment Marketization Instruction of learning		Meaning the same thing

It is extremely difficult to predict which combination of policies and practices will work everywhere because, as seen in Table 5.1, they are only comparable at the level of rhetoric; they are not transferable because, once they are adopted or adapted, they may lose their original meaning. Policies and practices cannot travel consistently because the factors and combinations that shape them in one place make it difficult to replicate them in another context. Thus, I would contend that international studies such as PISA or TIMSS are probably suited for comparability of students' performance, but not for transferability of policies.

There is convergence in policy 'talk' or the rhetoric of policies. There is also convergence in aspects such as selection of textbooks, autonomy of teachers or some freedom for principals in budget management. But even here, such freedom is limited since the budget management is constrained by the relatively small amount of funding available to principals. The question that now arises is whether less power brings about less accountability.

Furthermore, the convergence in school policies or practices, in textbooks, school materials and budget management are not seen as belonging only to the realm of high-performing countries.

Some proposals have theoretical or ideological neatness. Some people may like the idea, value or principle of free choice. Epistemic communities are harnessed by competition and marketization (neo-liberals)[2] or they take the public school idea as a value. Others favor welfare-based societies. However, very few, if any, have been able to harness consistent evidence to hold up their proposal as true in all places and systems. We end up with contrasting studies that show success for each approach in specific situations.

New pseudo-paradigms challenge the concepts of decentralization and autonomy of schools (some see them as a value), with a call for re-centralization and accountability of schools and policies. Even worse, evidence from the field research project presented in this study, and from many researchers before me, shows that decentralization and autonomy or supply-driven policies are promoted in different ways around systems, districts and schools.

Principals, teachers, representatives on boards, and local educational authorities will adjust or make sense of supply-driven policy or rules to suit their own culture, context, situation, politics (Steiner-Khamsi, 2003) or practice, and daily life.

Of these policies and rules imposed by higher central authorities (state or national), they will follow only those that make sense in their own microcosmic reality, namely the school. Even at the local level of analysis, this seems to be the case, as stated by Spillane:

> Inundated with signals from their environment, people notice some and ignore most others, as they use the lenses they have developed through experience to filter their awareness. Indeed, part of sense-making involves categorizing signals into some sort of framework (2004, pp.168-169).

In light of all of this, is there anything left for policy-makers?

---

[2] As defined by Arnove et al. (1997).

Policy Suggestions

The OECD seems to believe that there are best practices and benchmarks in policies and practices:

> Much as the development of macro economic models in the post World War Two period brought order and coherence to the debates on economic strategy, so the development of an analytic framework related to PISA that capitalizes on the natural variation in educational performance that can be observed across countries offers a similar prize in the arena of education policy (OECD 2006, p.5).

Relating education policy to economics may be presumptuous. It is fairly easy to measure economies by some conventions in national accounts. In education there is still debate over what education really means. If there is no agreement on what education is, how can there be agreement about how to measure it, assess it and improve it? Furthermore, supply-driven policies may increase the size of bureaucracies. i.e., inspectors and advisors to ensure that schools, principals and teachers implement policies the way the policy-makers intended. Policy-makers could move closer to demand-driven policies. Under this approach, incentives matter.

Policy-makers could also establish standards as targets, listen to local and school conditions and maneuver through incentives. Formulations, details and scope of school policies and practices would be left for the schools and their district authorities to decide. However, it is critical to realize that standards, targets and incentives have to be linked to differences in socio-economic levels, socio-cultural capitals, and school attainment by clusters. Once the indicators, benchmarks or standards have been established in certain subjects (such as mathematics, sciences, mother-tongue language and foreign languages) and levels of enrolment and retention have been set, the schools and their boards will be left to design, organize and implement policies and practices to suit their own conditions and culture. Then schools will be accountable for moving in a direction towards achievement.

Therefore, targets and accountability to the multi-layered and negotiated set of standards are the real policy instruments available to policy-makers where an ideal model would have the best possible teachers, principals and parents without a probable need for authorities as monitoring agents. However, the more realistic picture is a world often reduced to the chores of a daily, sometimes cumbersome, set of life tasks where principals, teachers and parents don't always behave in uniformly positive, altruistic ways.

Given the framework of the day-to-day life of schools, policy-makers are left with incentive-driven measures to promote change (or reassure behavior) so that the right policy–practice mix for each school, district or system flourishes. The correct mix of policies and practices for teaching and learning will flourish if national or state authorities set in place the right "mold" or set of institutional arrangements (Chubb & Moe 1990) or "basic principles" (Hanushek et al 1994) or "systemic conditions" (Darling-Hammond 2001) or initial conditions, as I call them. The system of school education has to change from a rule driven system to a system or systems of multi-layered and negotiated targets, standards (Ravitch 1995), accountability and incentives. In this sense the OECD's proposition of "policy drivers" (OECD 2006, pp.5-8) makes sense – but only as an analysis drawn from and directed to a situation in a given school education system.

Whether policy-makers end up designing or implementing national targets versus state targets, district targets or school targets is an issue of concern to each country, nation or system. Borrowing or lending in this case is as shaky as borrowing or lending at the level of decentralization or autonomy; many things are lost in translation (the Actor Network Theory – own translators' interpretations), or they may be wrongly communicated or misconstrued as with the "telephone game" cited by Spillane, (2004, p.xi).

It is desirable that targets are set in agreement and discussion with districts and schools, school by school so that the incentive response is tied to the achievement of the commonly set targets. Policy-makers could save resources spent in trying to implement prescribed policies and use them for incentives. International organizations such as the OECD can then focus their attention and scarce resources on developing instruments to compare, and transferring some inputs and outputs as suggested in Table 5.1. Investing in the transferability of policies, processes and practices has a much lower or maybe even negative return. Policy-makers may treat international studies such as PISA, TIMSS and PIRLS with the respect due when it comes to the comparability of some inputs and outputs. However, when interpretations of cause and effect relationships are raised, there is a need to exercise caution.

Table 5.2: Factors and combinations that may affect performance of students and schools

Levels (modes) of autonomy	Schools' organizational structures	Admission decision policy	Levels of authority deciding on admissions	Class groupings	Level of decision-making and power relationships inside the school	Power relationships outside the schools	Domains of decision-making	Systemic and cultural factors	Other factors
1) Full autonomy	1) Lower secondary schools only	1) Nearest school	1) Principals	1) Mixed ability	1) School Board dominant	1) Local authorities	1) Curriculum	1) National exams	1) School pedagogy (Montessori, Steiner–Waldorf, International Baccalaureate, other)
2) In consultation with others	2) Primary and lower secondary schools in the same premises	2) Free choice: first-come-first-served	2) Teachers	2) Students' own profile or school career decisions	2) District school board dominant inside the school	2) State authorities	2) Textbooks	2) Random exams	2) Socio-economic factors (student intake, school socio-economic background)
3) Within a framework	3) Lower secondary and upper secondary schools in the same premises	3) Limited free choice	3) Management teams	3) Grade point average from feeder school or lower grade level	3) Parents dominant	3) National authorities	3) School materials	3) Regional systems	3) Information and communications technology in schools
4) One or some of the above combined in full autonomy	4) Upper secondary schools only	4) Nearest school plus quota for free choice	4) Guidance or pastoral teachers	4) At random	4) Teachers dominant	4) Strong superintendent or education chief	4) School equipment	4) Federal systems	4) Teaching and learning methods

Levels (modes) of autonomy	Schools' organizational structures	Admission decision policy	Levels of authority deciding on admissions	Class groupings	Level of decision-making and power relationships inside the school	Power relationships outside the schools	Domains of decision-making	Systemic and cultural factors	Other factors
5) One or some of the above in consultation with others	5) Primary and lower and upper secondary schools in the same premises	5) Nearest school plus supply/ demand balance	5) School boards	5) By alphabetical order	5) Young principals with new agenda	5) Weak superintendent or education chief	5) Time-tabling	5) Parliament or congress members involved	5) Other school policies and practices: uniforms, single-sex, lunches, praying
6) Two or more of the above by consensus	6) Lower secondary schools of four years	6) Siblings in the school	6) One or some of the above plus parents	6) Student's behavior record	6) Retiring principals with no agenda	6) Inspectors and supervisors	6) Exams/ tests	6) Level of expenditure	6) Disciplinary policies inside and outside the classrooms
7) Other	7) Lower secondary schools of three years	7) Feeder school's recommendations	7) Teachers from lower ISCED level school	7) Students' gender balance	7) Strong principals	7) Elected school boards	7) Meeting with parents	7) Strong versus weak unions	7) Professional development policies
	8) Lower secondary (intermediate) schools of two years only	8) Ballot system based on an array of criteria	8) Teachers from upper ISCED level school	8) Students with friends	8) Superintendent or local education chief dominant inside the school	8) Political appointees in local authority	8) Course curriculum	8) Red-tape culture	8) Students' own abilities and attitudes
	9) Upper secondary schools of two years	9) Academic merits of students; exams, GPA	9) A combination of two or more from above	9) Students' home addresses (so they can travel together)	9) Unions' presence inside the school	9) Teachers' unions	9) Self-evaluating/ assessment of students	9) Teacher profession valued	9) Full-day schools
	10) Upper secondary schools of three years	10) Religious affiliation		10) Ability segmentation	10) Students' participation in School Boards (decision-making boards)	10) Principals' unions	10) Innovation	10) Large versus small schools	10) Ethos in the school and in the classroom

Levels (modes) of autonomy	Schools' organizational structures	Admission decision policy	Levels of authority deciding on admissions	Class groupings	Level of decision-making and power relationships inside the school	Power relationships outside the schools	Domains of decision-making	Systemic and cultural factors	Other factors
	11) Upper secondary schools of four years	11) Religious acceptance		11) Combination of two or more from above	11) Church-related organizations (archdioceses)	11) Parents' associations	11) Self-evaluation of teachers	11) Competitive culture	11) Size of classroom
	12) Schools with two years of primary education and four years of secondary education	12) Different combinations of two or more factors from above			12) Principals with or without open-door policy	12) Professional associations	12) Budgets	12) National standards	12) Planning and organizational policies
	13) Schools with two years of primary education and six years of secondary education	13) Interviews with parents and children			13) Teachers with or without open-door policies	13) NGO's	13) Strategic planning	13) State or district standards	13) Transparency values of society
	14) Upper secondary schools attached to colleges	14) Persuading Interviews			14) School with department heads or faculty heads	14) Principals' styles, personal connections and power relations	14) Hiring teachers	14) Content-based curriculum	14) Structure of personnel (by age and experience of teachers)
	15) Upper secondary schools for the talented in science and technology	15) Proxies for interviews			15) School with deputy principals or vice-principals and schools without them		15) Firing or removing teachers	15) Goal-oriented curriculum	15) Level of training of teachers

Levels (modes) of autonomy	Schools' organizational structures	Admission decision policy	Levels of authority deciding on admissions	Class groupings	Level of decision-making and power relationships inside the school	Power relationships outside the schools	Domains of decision-making	Systemic and cultural factors	Other factors
	16) Secondary schools with all sorts of sizes, streams and/or specializations (vocational, technical, general)				16) Clusters or groups of schools per district		16) Salaries of teachers	16) Large education systems or districts	16) Open-door schools
	17) Lower secondary schools and upper secondary schools with specializations in arts or music, or languages.						17) Hiring or removing principals	17) School and education-prone culture	17) Schools with or without police presence
	18) Shared or borrowed facilities						18) Salaries of principals	18) Education of parents	18) Different architectural designs and decorations

References

Aho, Erkki; Pitkänen, Kari & Sahlberg, Pasi (2006): 'Policy Development and Reform Principles of Basic and Secondary Education in Finland since 1968.' In *Education Working Paper* Series 2: The World Bank. Retrieved on August 28, 2006 from http://web.worldbank.org/wbsite/external/topics/exteducation/0,,contentmdk:20442088~menupk:282405~pagepk:1 48956~pipk:216618~theSitepk:282386,00.html.

Alberta Education (2006): Preliminary Student Population by Grade, School and Authority, Alberta: 2005/2006 School Year. Alberta, Canada: Information Services Branch. Retrieved on July 15, 2006 from http://www.education. gov.ab.ca/ei/statistics/population.asp.

Alexander, Robin J. (2000): *Culture and Pedagogy: International Comparisons in Primary Education.* United Kingdom: Blackwell Publishing.

Alexander, Robin J. (2001): 'Border Crossings: Towards a Comparative Pedagogy.' In *Comparative Education* 37 (4): pp.507-523.

Andere, Eduardo M. (2003): *La Educación en México: un Fracaso Monumental [Education in Mexico: A Monumental Failure].* Mexico DF: Temas de Hoy. Editorial Planeta Mexicana.

Andere, Eduardo M. (2006): *México Sigue en Riesgo: El Monumental Reto de la Educación. [Mexico Still at Risk: The Monumental Challenge of Education].* México DF: Temas de Hoy. Editorial Planeta Mexicana.

Andere, Eduardo M. (2007): 'Las Leyes, la Política y la Alta Política Educativa'.*[Law, Politics and Higher Education Policy] Cuestiones Constitucionales*: México DF: UNAM: pp.3-42.

Arnaut, Albert (1998): *La Federalización Educativa en México. Historia del Debate sobre la Centralización y la Descentralización Educativa (1889-1994). [The Federalization of education in Mexico: History of the Debate about Education Centralization and Decentralization (1889-1994)].* México: El Colegio de México-CIDE.

Arnove, Robert F. (1980): 'Comparative Education and World-Systems Analysis.' In *Comparative Education Review* 24 (1): pp.48-62.

Arnove, Robert F.; Torres, Carlos Alberto; Franz, Stephen & Morse, Kimberly (1997): 'A Political Sociology of Education and Development in Latin America: The Conditioned State, Neoliberalism, and Educational Policy.' In Bradshaw, York W. (ed.) *Education in Comparative Perspective: New Lessons from Around the World.* Leiden, Netherlands: E.J. Brill, pp.140-158.

Astiz, M. Fernanda; Wiseman, Alexander W. & Baker, David P. (2002): 'Slouching towards Decentralization: Consequences of Globalization for Curricular Control in National Education Systems.' In *Comparative Education Review* 46 (1): pp.66-88.

Ball, Stephen J (1998): 'Big Policies/Small World: An Introduction to International Perspectives in Education Policy.' In *Comparative Education* 34 (2): pp.119-130.

Baker, David P. & LeTendre, Gerald K. (2005): *National Differences, Global*

Similarities. World Culture and the Future of Schooling. Stanford: Stanford University Press.

Bjork, Christopher (2003): 'Local Responses to Decentralization Policy in Indonesia.' In *Comparative Education Review* 47 (2): pp.184-216.

Boli, John; Ramirez, Franciso O. & Meyer, John W (1985): 'Explaining the Origins and Expansion of Mass Education.' In *Comparative Education Review* 29 (2): pp.145-170.

Bonnet, Gérard (2002): 'Reflections in a Critical Eye [1]: On the Pitfalls of International Assessment. Knowledge and Skills for Life: First Results from PISA 2000.' Review essay. In *Assessment in Education: Principles, Policy and Practice.* 9 (3): pp.387-398.

Boston, Jonathan; Martin, John; Pallot, June & Walsh, Pat (1996): *Public Management: The New Zealand Model.* Auckland, New Zealand: Oxford University Press.

Bray, Mark & Thomas R. Murray (1995): 'Levels of Comparison in Educational Studies: Different Insights from Different Literatures and the Value of Multi-level Analyses.' In *Harvard Educational Review* 65 (3): pp.472-490.

Bray, Mark & Mukundan, M.V. (2003): *Management and Governance for EFA: Is Decentralisation Really an Answer?* Hong Kong: Comparative Education Research Centre, Faculty of Education, University of Hong Kong. Retrieved on May 09, 2006 from http://portal.unesco.org/education/en/file_download.php/5ac6f3ae42ac5be976b6d1bc870708e1Management+and+governance+for+EFA.+Is+decentralization+really+the+answer.doc.

Bray, Mark (2003): 'Control of Education: Issues and Tensions in Centralization and Decentralization.' In Arnove, Robert F. & Torres, Carlos Alberto (eds): *Comparative Education: The Dialectics of the Global and the Local*, 2nd edition. Lanham, Maryland: Rowman & Littlefield Publishers. pp.204-228.

Brickman, William W. (1965): 'Prehistory of Comparative Education to the End of the Eighteenth Century.' In *Comparative Education Review* 10 (4): pp.30-47.

Broadfoot, Patricia (1999): 'Stones from Other Hills may Serve to Polish the Jade of this One: Towards a Neo-comparative "Learnology" of Education.' In *Compare* 29 (3): pp.217-231.

Broadfoot, Patricia (2001): 'Editorial. Culture, Learning and Comparative Education.' In *Comparative Education* 37 (3): pp.261-266.

Broadfoot, Patricia (2003a): 'Editorial. Complex Cultural Molecules: Towards a "Chemistry" of Comparative Education.' In *Comparative Education* 39 (1): pp.3-5.

Broadfoot, Patricia (2003b): 'Editorial. Post-Comparative Education?' In *Comparative Education* 39 (3): pp.275-278.

Broadfoot, Patricia (2003c): 'Editorial. Globalisation in Comparative Perspective: Macro and Micro.' In *Comparative Education* 39 (4): pp.411-413.

Brown, Phillip & Lauder, Hugh (1996): 'Education, Globalization and Economic development.' In *Journal of Education Policy* 11 (1): pp.1-25.

Bruner, Jerome (1996): *The Culture of Education.* Cambridge, Massachusetts: Harvard University Press.

Bussière, Patrick; Cartwright, Fernando & Knighton, Tamara (2004): *The Performance of Canada's Youth in Mathematics, Reading, Science and Problem Solving: 2003 First Findings for Canadians Aged 15*. Ottawa, Canada: Statistics Canada, Human Resources and Skills Development Canada Council of Ministers of Education. Series. Retrieved on July 15, 2006 from http://www.pisa.gc.ca/publications_e.shtml.

Callon, M. (1986): 'Some Elements of a Sociology of Translation: Domestication of the Scallops and the Fishermen of St Brieuc Bay.' In Law, John (ed.), *Power, Action and Belief. A New Sociology of Knowledge?* London: Routledge & Kegan Paul. pp.196-233.

Carnoy, Martin & Rhoten, Diana (2002): 'What does Globalization Mean for Educational Change? A Comparative Approach.' In *Comparative Education* 46 (1): pp.1-9.

Carter, David S.G. & O'Neill, Marnie H. (1995): *International Perspectives on Educational Reform and Policy Implementation*. Great Britain: The Falmer Press, Taylor & Francis Group

Cheung, Wing-Leong & Sidhu, Ravinder (2003): 'A Tale of Two Cities: Education Responds to Globalisation in Hong Kong and Singapore in the Aftermath of the Asian Economic Crisis.' In *Asia Pacific Journal of Education* 23 (1): pp.43-68.

Chubb, John E. & Moe, Terry M. (1990): *Politics, Markets and America's Schools*. Washington DC: The Brookings Institution.

Coleman, James S.; Campbell, Ernest; Hobson, Carol; McPartland, James; Mood, Alexander; Weinfeld, Frederick & York, Robert (1979): *Equality of Educational Opportunity*. Reprint of 1966 edition published by US Office of Education. Washington: Arno Press Collection, Perennial Works in Sociology. New York: Arno Press Inc.

'Comunicación Social de la Secretaría de Educación Pública.' (2006): Alcanza México las Metas del Milenio en Educación. Retrieved on February 14, 2006 from http://www.sep.org.mx.

Coulby, David; Cowen, Robert & Jones, Crispin (eds.) (2000): *Education in Times of Transition. World Yearbook of Education 2000*. London: Kogan Page.

Cowen, Robert: (2003): 'Editorial. Post-comparative Education?' In *Comparative Education* 39 (3): pp.275-278.

Crossley, Michael (1999): 'Reconceptualising Comparative and International Education.' In *Compare* 29 (3): pp.249-267.

Crossley, Michael (2000): 'Bridging Cultures and Traditions in the Reconceptualisation of Comparative and International Education.' In *Comparative Education* 36 (3): pp.319-232.

Crossley, Michael & Jarvis, Peter (2001): 'Context Matters.' In *Comparative Education* 37 (4): pp.405-408.

Crossley, Michael & Keith Watson (2003): *Comparative and International Research in Education: Globalisation, context and difference*. London: Routledge Falmer, Taylor & Francis Group.

Cuéllar-Marchelli, Helga (2002): 'Decentralization and Privatization of Education in El Salvador: Assessing the Experience.' In *International Journal of Educational Development* 23 (2): pp.145-166.

Czarniawska, Barbara & Sevón, Guje (1996): *Translating Organizational Change*. Berlin: Walter de Gruyter.

Czarniawska, Barbara (1998): *A Narrative Approach to Organization Studies*. Qualitative Research Methods Vol. 43. Thousand Oaks, California: Sage Publications.

Czarniawska, Barbara & Sevón, Guje (2005): *Global Ideas: How Ideas, Objects and Practices Travel in the Global Economy*. Sweden: Liber & Copenhagen Business School Press. Advances in Organization Studies Series.

Dale, Roger (1994): 'The McDonaldisation of Schooling and the Street-level Bureaucrat.' In *Curriculum Studies* 2 (2): pp.249-262.

Dale, Roger (1997): 'The State and the Governance of Education: An Analysis of the Restructuring of the State–Education Relationship.' In Halsey, A.H.; Lauder, Hugh; Brown, Phillip & Wells, Amy Stuart (eds.), *Education: Culture, Economy, and Society*. Oxford: Oxford University Press, pp.273-282.

Dale, Roger (1999): 'Specifying Globalization Effects on National Policy: A Focus on the Mechanisms.' In *Journal of Education Policy* 14 (1): pp.1-17.

Dale, Roger (2000): 'Globalization and Education: Demonstrating a "Common World Educational Culture" or Locating a "Globally Structured Educational Agenda"?' In *Education Theory* 50(4): pp.427-448.

Dale, Roger (2001): 'Constructing a Long Spoon for Comparative Education: Charting the Career of the "New Zealand model".' In *Comparative Education* 37 (4): pp.493-500.

Dale, Roger (2005): 'Globalization, knowledge economy and comparative education.' Introductory article: In *Comparative Education Review* 41 (2): pp.117-149.

Dale, Roger (2006): 'From Comparison to Translation: Extending the Research Imagination? In *Globalisation, Societies and Education* 4 (2): pp.179-192.

Dale, Roger & Robertson, Susan L. (2002): 'The Varying Effects of Regional Organizations as Subjects of Globalization of Education.' In *Comparative Education Review* 46 (1): pp.10-36.

Darling-Hammond, Linda (2001): *El Derecho de Aprender: Crear buenas escuelas para todos*. Barcelona: Editorial Ariel. [Published in English in 1997: *The Right to Learn: A Blueprint for Creating Schools that Work.* Jossey-Bass. A Wiley company.]

Davies, Scott & Guppy, Neil (1997): 'Globalization and Educational Reforms in Anglo-American Democracies.' In *Comparative Education Review* 41 (4): pp.435-459.

di Gropello, Emiliana (2004): 'Education Decentralization and Accountability Relationships in Latin America.' World Bank Policy Research Working Paper No. 3453 (November 10, 2004). Retrieved on May 19, 2006 from http://papers.ssrn.com/sol3/papers.cfm?abstract_id=625333.

Dyer, Caroline (1999): 'Researching the Implementation of Educational Policy: A Backward Mapping Approach.' In *Comparative Education* 35 (1): pp.45-61.

Epstein, Erwin H. (1992): 'The Problematic Meaning of "Comparison" in

Comparative Education.' In Schriewer, Jürgen & Holmes, Brian (eds.), *Theories and Methods in Comparative Education.* 3rd edition. Frankfurt am Main: Peter Lang Publishing.

Finnemore, Martha (1993): 'International Organizations as Teachers of Norms: The United Nations Scientific, Educational, and Cultural Organization and Science Policy.' In *International Organization* 47 (4): pp.565-497.

Fiske, Edward B. (1996): *Decentralization of Education: Politics and Consensus. Directions in Development.* Washington DC: The World Bank. Retrieved on May 12, 2006 from http://siteresources.worldbank.org/ EDUCATION/Resources/278200-099079877269/5476641099080000281/ Dec_education_politics_consensus_EN96.pdf.

Fiske, Edward B. & Ladd, Helen F. (2000): *When Schools Compete: A Cautionary Tale.* Washington DC: Brookings Institution Press.

Gershberg, Alec Ian (1999): 'Education "Decentralization" Processes in Mexico and Nicaragua: Legislative versus Ministry-Led Reform Strategies.' In *Comparative Education* 31 (1): pp.63-80.

Gibton, Dan; Sabar, Naama & Goldring, Ellen B. (2000): 'How Principals of Autonomous Schools in Israel View Implementation of Decentralization and Restructuring Policy: Risks, Rights and Wrongs.' In *Educational Evaluation and Policy Analysis* 22 (2): pp.193-210.

Gittell, Marilyn (1972): 'Decentralization and Citizen Participation in Education.' In *Public Administration Review* 32: pp.670-686.

Goldstein, Harvey (2004a): 'International Comparisons of Student Attainment: Some Issues Arising from the PISA Study.' In *Assessment in Education: Principles, Policy and Practice.* 11 (39): pp.319-330.

Goldstein, Harvey (2004b): 'The Education World Cup: International Comparisons of Student Achievement.' Plenary talk to Association for Educational Assessment – Europe: Budapest Nov. 4-6, 2004. Mimeo.

Gopinathan, Saravanan (2001): 'Globalisation, the State and Education Policy in Singapore. In Tan, Jason; Gopinathan, Saravanan & Ho, Wah Kam (eds.), *Challenges Facing the Singapore Education System Today.* Singapore: Prentice Hall.

Gopinathan, Saravanan (2006): 'School Effectiveness and School Improvement in Singapore: An East Asian Perspective.' In Lee, John & Williams, Michael (eds.), *School Improvement: International Perspectives.* New York: Nova Science Publishers, pp.213-226.

Gorard, Stephen (2001): 'International Comparisons of School Effectiveness: The Second Component of the "Crisis Account" in England.' In *Comparative Education* 37 (3): pp.279-296.

Grant, Nigel (2000): 'Tasks for Comparative Education in the New Millennium.' In *Comparative Education* 36 (3): pp.309-317.

Green, Andy (1997): 'Educational Achievement in Centralized and Decentralized Systems.' In Halsey, A.H.; Lauder, Hugh; Brown, Phillip & Wells, Amy Stuart (eds.), *Education: Culture, Economy, and Society.* Oxford: Oxford University Press, pp.283-298.

Grindle, Merilee S. (2002): Interest, Institutions, and Reformers: The Politics of Education decentralization in Mexico. PDF Draft. Available at: http://

www.wilsoncenter.org/topics/docs/Grindle_Paper.pdf.

Grindle, Merilee S. (2006): 'Producing Ambiguous Outcomes: Education Reform in the Context of Decentralization.' In Abel, Christopher & Lewis, Colin (eds), *Developments in Public Sector Management in Latin America*. (Forthcoming)

Guevara, Niebla Gilberto (2006): 'Democracia y Educación: Dos Notas Críticas.' [Democracy and Education: Two Critical Notes]. In *Revista Mexicana de Investigación Educativa* [Mexican Journal of Education Research]. 11 (29): pp.639-653.

Guichard, Stéphanie (2005): 'The Education Challenge in Mexico: Delivering Good Quality Education to All.' Economics Department Working Paper, No. 447, ECO/WKP 34 (September).

Hall, Gene E. & Carter, David S.G. (1995): 'Implementing Change in the 1990s: Paradigms, Practices and Possibilities. Epilogue: Carter, David S.G. & O'Neill, Marnie H. (eds.), *International Perspectives on Educational Reform and Policy Implementation*. Great Britain: The Falmer Press, Taylor & Francis Group.

Hallak, Jacques (2000): 'Globalisation and its Impact on Education.' In Mebrahtu, Teame; Crossley, Michael & Johnson, David (eds.), *Globalisation, Educational Transformation and Societies in Transition*. Oxford: Symposium Books. pp.21-40.

Halls, W.D. (1997): 'Comparative Studies in Education, 1964-1977: A Personal View.' In *Comparative Education* 13 (2): pp.81-86.

Hanushek, Eric A. with Benson, Charles S.; Freeman, Richard B.; Jamison, Dean T.; Levin, Henry M.; Maynard, Rebecca A.; Murnane, Richard J.; Rivkin, Steven G.; Sabot, Richard H.; Solmon, Lewis C.; Summers, Anita A.; Welch, Finis & Wolfe, Barbara L. (1994): *Making Schools Work: Improving Performance and Controlling Costs*. Washington DC: The Brookings Institution.

Hargreaves, Andy (2003): *Teaching in the Knowledge Society: Education in the Age of Insecurity*. New York: Teachers College Press.

Hartley, David (2003): 'Education as a Global Positioning Device: Some Theoretical Considerations.' In *Comparative Education* 9 (4): pp.439-450.

Heckman, James J. & Masterov, V. Dimitriy (2007): 'The Productivity Argument for Investing in Children.' *Discussion Paper No. 2725*. Germany: The Institute for the Study of Labor (IZA): pp.1-100.

Hedmo, Tina; Sahlin-Andersson, Kerstin & Wedlin, Linda (2005): 'Fields of Imitation: The Global Expansion of Management Education.' In Czarniawska, Barbara & Sevón, Guje (eds.), *Global Ideas: How Ideas, Objects and Practices Travel in the Global Economy*. Advances in Organization Studies Series. Sweden: Liber & Copenhagen Business School Press.

Hopkins, David (2004): 'Improving the Quality of Education for All as an "Authentic" School Improvement Program.' In Lee, John Chi-kin; Lo, Leslie Nai-kwai & Walker, Allan (eds.), *Partnership and Change: Toward School Development*. Hong Kong: The Chinese University Press & Hong Kong Institute of Educational Research, pp.81-114.

Hopper, Earl I. (1968): 'A Typology for the Classification of Educational Systems.' In *Sociology* 2 (1): pp.29-46.

Hoxby, Caroline M. (2001): 'If Families Matter Most, Where Do Schools Come In?' In Moe, Terry M. (ed.), *A Primer on America's Schools*. Stanford, California: Hoover Institution Press.

Imam, Syeda Rumnaz (2005): 'English as a Global Language and the Question of Nation-Building Education in Bangladesh.' In *Comparative Education* 41 (4): pp.471-486.

Jakobi, Anja (2006): 'The Internationality of Lifelong Learning.' In Rinne, Risto & Kallo, Johanna (eds.), *Supranational Regimes and National Education Policies – Encountering Challenge*. Helsinki: Finnish Educational Research Association, (Forthcoming).

Johnson, David; Smith, Bob & Crossley, Michael (eds.) (1998): *Learning and Teaching in an International Context: Research, Theory and Practice*. Bristol: Bristol Papers in Education: Comparative International Studies.

Kamens, David H.; Meyer, John W. & Benavot, Aaron (1996): 'Worldwide Patterns in Academic Secondary Education Curricula.' In *Comparative Education Review* 40 (29): pp.116-138.

Kaufman, Herbert (1969): 'Administrative Decentralization and Political Power.' In *Public Administration Review* 29 (1): pp.3-15.

Kaufman, Robert R. & Nelson, Joan M. (2005): 'Políticas de Reforma Educativa: Comparación entre Países.' [Education Reform Policies: Country Comparisons]. In *PREAL (Programa de Promoción de la Reforma Educativa en América Latina y el Caribe: Partnership for Educational Revitalization in the Americas)* No. 33. Retrieved on April 08, 2006 from www.preal.org.

King, Edmund (1989): 'Comparative Investigation of Education: An Evolutionary Process.' In *Prospects* XIX (3).

Kirp, David L. (2006): 'Idea Lab: After the Bell Curve.' In *New York Times*: July 23, 2006.

Latour, Bruno (1986): 'The Powers of Association.' In Law, John (ed.), *Power, Action and Belief. A New Sociology of Knowledge?* London: Routledge & Kegan Paul, pp.265-280.

Latour, Bruno (1988): *The Pasteurization of France*. Cambridge, Mass.: Harvard University Press.

Latour, Bruno (2005): *Reassembling the Social: An Introduction to Actor-Network-Theory*. Great Britain: Oxford University Press.

Lavonen, Jari (2006): 'Education Policy behind Success of Finnish Students in PISA 2003: Scientific Literacy Assessment.' Paper presented in the International Symposium on Primary Education. April 15, 2006. Izmir, Turkey: Mimeo.

Law, John (1986a): 'Power/Knowledge and the Dissolution of the Sociology of Knowledge.' Editor's introduction: Law, John (ed.), *Power, Action and Belief. A New Sociology of Knowledge?* London: Routledge & Kegan Paul, pp.1-19.

Law, John (1986b): 'On the Methods of Long Distance Control: Vessels, Navigation and the Portuguese Route to India.' In Law, John (ed.), *Power,*

Action and Belief. A New Sociology of Knowledge? The Sociological Review: Sociological Review Monograph 32. London: Routledge & Kegan Paul, pp.234-263.

Lee, Chong Jae (2005): 'The Korean Equalization Trap.' President of Korean Educational Development Institute. Retrieved on December 15, 2005 from http://eng.kedi.re.kr/.

Levin, Benjamin (1998): 'An Epidemic of Education Policy: (What) Can We Learn from Each Other?' In *Comparative Education* 34 (2): pp.131-141.

Levin, Henry M. (2005): Foreword. In Scott, Janelle T. (ed.), *School Choice and Diversity: What the Evidence Says*. New York: Teachers College Press. pp.vii-viii.

Levin, Henry M. & Kelley, Carolyn (1994): 'Can Education Do It Alone?' In *Economics of Education Review*. 13 (29): pp.97-108.

Lindblad, Sverker & Popkewitz, Thomas S. (2004a): 'Introduction: Educational Restructuring: (Re)Thinking the Problematic of Reform'. In Lindblad, Sverker & Popkewitz, Thomas S. (eds.), *Educational Restructuring: International Perspectives of Traveling Policies*. Connecticut: Information Age Publishing Inc., pp.vii-xxxi.

Lindblad, Sverker & Popkewitz, Thomas S. (2004b): 'Governance in the Narratives of Progress and Denials.' In Lindblad, Sverker & Popkewitz, Thomas S. (eds.), *Educational Restructuring: International Perspectives of Traveling Policies*. Connecticut: Information Age Publishing Inc. pp.69-94.

Little, Angela (2000): 'Development Studies and Comparative Education: Context, Content, Comparison and Contributors.' In *Comparative Education* 36 (3): pp.279-296.

McGinn, Noel F. (1996): 'Education, Democratization, and Globalization: A Challenge for Comparative Education.' In *Comparative Education Review* 40 (4): pp.342-357.

McGinn, Noel & Street, Susan (1986): 'Educational Decentralization: Weak State or Strong State?' In *Comparative Education Review* 30 (4): pp.471-490.

McMeeking, Robert W. (2004): 'Chile Vouchers and Beyond.' In Rotberg, Iris C. (ed.), *Balancing Change and Transition in Global Education Reform*. Maryland: Scarecrow Education.

McNeely, Connie L. & Cha, Yun-Kyung (1994): 'Worldwide Educational Convergence through International Organizations: Avenues for Research.' In *Education Policy Analysis Archives* 2, No. 14 (November 29, 1994). Retrieved on March 1, 2006 from http://epaa.asu.edu/epaa/v2n14.html.

McNeely, Connie L. (1995): 'Prescribing National Education Policies: The Role of International Organizations.' In *Comparative Education Review* 39 (4): pp.483-507.

Meyer, John W.; Boli, John; Thomas, George M. & Ramirez, Francisco O. (1997): 'World Society and the Nation-State.' In *The American Journal of Sociology* 103 (1): pp.144-181.

Mok, Ka-ho (2004): *Education Reform and Education Policy in East Asia*. Hong Kong: Comparative Education Policy Research Unit.

Mok, Joshua Ka-ho & Chan, David Kin-keung (2002): *Globalization and Education: The Quest for Quality Education in Hong Kong*. Hong Kong: Hong Kong University Press.

Mok, Ka-Ho & Tan, Jason (2004): *Globalization and Marketization in Education: A Comparative Analysis of Hong Kong and Singapore*. UK: Edward Elgar.

Mortimore, Peter (1998): *The Road to Improvement: Reflections on School Effectiveness*. The Netherlands: Swets and Zeitlinger Publishers.

Mortimore, Peter (2001): 'Globalisation, Effectiveness and Improvement' In *School Effectiveness and School Improvement* 12 (1): pp.229-249.

Mukundan, M.V. & Bray, Mark (2004): 'The Decentralisation of Education in Kerala State, India: Rhetoric and Reality.' In *International Review of Education* 50: pp.223-243.

Mullis, Ina V.S.; Martin, Michael O.; Gonzalez, Eugenio J. & Chrostowski, Steve J. (2004): *TIMSS 2003 International Mathematics Report: Findings from IEA's Trends in International Mathematics and Science Study at the Fourth and Eighth Grades*. Chestnut Hill, Massachusetts: International Association for the Evaluation of Educational Achievement and TIMSS & PIRLS International Study Center, Lynch School of Education, Boston College.

National Center for Education Statistics (2001): *Digest of Education Statistics, 2001*: Chapter 2. 'Elementary and Secondary Education.' Retrieved on December 9, 2002 from http://nces.ed.gov/pubs2002/digest2001/tables/dt089.asp and June 20, 2006 from http://nces.ed.gov/programs/digest/d05/tables/dt05_084.asp.

New Zealand Ministry of Education (2001): *Schooling in New Zealand: A Guide*. Wellington: Ministry of Education. Retrieved on June 27, 2006 from http://www.minedu.govt.nz/web/downloadable/dl6169_v1/schooling-in-nz---final-july-2003.pdf.

New Zealand Ministry of Education (2005): 'School Type as at 1 July 2005.' From *Education Counts* on edCentre. Retrieved on June 27 06 from http://educationcounts.edcentre.govt.nz/statistics/schooling/school-type-at-july-2005.html.

Ninnes, Peter & Burnett, Gregory: 'Comparative Education Research: Post-structuralist Possibilities [1]' In *Comparative Education* 39 (3): pp.279-297.

Noah, Harold J. (1986): 'The Use and Abuse of Comparative Education.' In Altbach, Philip G. & Kelly, Gail P. (eds.), *New Approaches to Comparative Education*. Chicago: University of Chicago Press.

Novoa, Antonio & Yariv-Mashal, Tali (2003): 'Comparative Research in Education: A Mode of Governance or a Historical Journey?' In *Comparative Education* 39 (4): pp.423-438.

Olds, Kris (2005): 'Articulating Agendas and Traveling Principles in the Layering of New Strands of Academic Freedom in Contemporary Singapore.' In Czarniawska, Barbara & Sevón, Guje (eds.), *Global Ideas: How Ideas, Objects and Practices Travel in the Global Economy*. Sweden: Liber & Copenhagen Business School Press. Advances in Organization Studies Series.

Olivera, Carlos E. (1992): 'Comparative Education: What Kind of Knowledge?' In Schriewer, Jürgen & Holmes, Brian (eds.), *Theories and Methods in Comparative Education*. 3rd edition. Frankfurt am Main; Bern; New York; Paris: Peter Lang Publishing.

O'Neill, Marnie (1995): Introduction: Carter, David S.G. & O'Neill, Marnie H., *International Perspectives on Educational Reform and Policy Implementation*. Great Britain: The Falmer Press, Taylor & Francis Group.

Organisation for Economic Co-operation and Development (1992): *Education at a Glance: OECD Indicators*. Paris. OECD Review Panel.

Organisation for Economic Co-operation and Development (1996): 'Shaping the 21st Century: The Contribution of Development Co-operation.' DAC (Development Assistance Committee). Retrieved on April 4, 2006 from http://oecd.org/dataoecd/23/35/2508761.dpf.

Organisation for Economic Co-operation and Development (1998): *Education at a Glance: OECD Indicators*. Paris. OECD Review Panel.

Organisation for Economic Co-operation and Development (2001): *Knowledge and Skills for Life: First Results from OECD Programme for International Student Assessment (PISA) 2000:* Paris.

Organisation for Economic Co-operation and Development (2003a): 'Indicators of National Education Systems: Locus of Decision-Making Questionnaire': *Education Secretariat*, (NW C 03-020): Mimeo.

Organisation for Economic Co-operation and Development (2003b): 'Data Collection Manual: Decision-Making in Education': *Education Secretariat*, titled (NW C 03-019): Mimeo.

Organisation for Economic Co-operation and Development (2004a): *Learning for Tomorrow's World: First Results from PISA 2003*. Paris.

Organisation for Economic Co-operation and Development (2004b): *Education at a Glance: OECD Indicators 2004*. Paris.

Organisation for Economic Co-operation and Development (2005a): 'Mexico: Assessment and Recommendations.' In *OECD Economic Surveys*. Paris.

Organisation for Economic Co-operation and Development (2005b): 'School Factors Related to Quality and Equity: Results from PISA 2000.' Retrieved on July 16, 2006 from http://www.pisa.oecd.org/document/35/0,2340,en_32252351_32236159_34669667_1_1_1_1,00.html.

Organisation for Economic Co-operation and Development (2006): 'Policy Implications of PISA: Proposal for a New System of Analytical Work.' Directorate for Education, Programme for International Student Assessment. EDU/PISA/GB(2006)5. 15-Feb-2006. 21st meeting of the PISA Governing Board: Seoul, March 6-8, 2006.

Organización para la Cooperación y el Desarrollo Económicos [Organisation for Economic Co-operation and Development]. 2004. 'Revisión de Políticas Nacionales de Educación: Chile.' [Review of National Policies of Education: Chile]. Paris: Centro para la Cooperación con los Países no Miembros de la OCDE [Centre for non-OECD Members Co-operation]. Paris.

Ornelas, Carlos. 1998. 'La Descentralización de la Educación en México: El Federalismo Difícil [Decentralization of Education in Mexico: The

Difficult Federalism]. In Cabrero, Enrique (ed.), *Las Políticas Decentralizadoras en México: Logros y Desencantos [Decentralization Policies in Mexico: Achievements and Pitfalls]*. México, DF: Miguel Angel Porrúa.

Ouchi, William G. & Segal, Lydia G. (2003): *Making Schools Work: A Revolutionary Plan to Get Your Children the Education They Need*. New York, NY: Simon & Schuster.

Peddie, Roger A. (1991): 'Comparative Studies in Education: Lessons for New Zealand?' New Zealand Planning Council: Education Models from Overseas. Seminar papers. Wellington.

Phillips, David (1989): 'Neither a Borrower nor a Lender Be? The Problems of Cross-National Attraction in Education.' In *Comparative Education* 25 (3): pp.267-274.

Phillips, David (2004): 'Toward a Theory of Policy Attraction in Education' In Steiner-Khamsi, Gita (ed.), *The Global Politics of Educational Borrowing and Lending*. New York: Teachers College Columbia University Press. pp.54-67.

Phillips, David & Ochs, Kimberly (2003): 'Processes of Policy Borrowing in Education: Some Explanatory and Analytical Devices.' In *Comparative Education* 39 (4): pp.451-461.

Phillips, David & Ochs, Kimberly (eds) (2004): *Educational Policy Borrowing: Historical Perspectives*. Oxford, UK: Oxford Studies in Comparative Education. Oxford: Symposium Books.

Popkewitz, Thomas P. (1996): 'Rethinking Decentralization and State/Civic Society Distinctions: The State as a Problematic of Governing.' In *Journal of Education Policy* 11 (1): pp.27-51.

Porter, Andrew C. & Gamoran, Adam (2002): 'Progress and Challenges for Large-Scale Studies.' In Porter, A.C. & Gamoran, A. (eds.), *Methodological Advances in Cross-National Surveys of Educational Achievement*. National Research Council, Board on International Comparative Studies in Education, Board on Testing and Assessment, Center for Education, Division of Behavioral and Social Sciences and Education. Washington, DC: National Academy Press. pp.3-23

Posner, Charles M. (2002): 'Education and the Philanthropic Ogre.' In *Comparative Education* 38 (4): pp.401-414.

Prais, S.J. (2003) 'Cautions on OECD's Recent Educational Survey (PISA).' In *Oxford Review of Education* 29 (2): pp.139-163.

Ravitch, Diane (1995): *National Standards in American Education: A Citizen's Guide*. Washington, D.C.: The Brookings Institution.

Reimers, Fernando (2002): 'La Lucha por la Igualdad de Oportunidades Educativas en América Latina como Proceso Político.' [The Fight for Equality in Education Opportunities in Latin America as a Political Process]. In *Revista Latinoamericana de Estudios Educativos* XXXII (001): pp.9-70.

Reynolds, David; Creemers, Bert; Stringfield, Sam; Teddlie, Charles; Schaffer, Gene & Bellin, Wynford (2002): *World Class Schools: International Perspectives on School Effectiveness*. London: Routledge/Falmer.

Ritzer, George (2004): *The McDonaldization of Society*. Revised New Century

Edition. Thousand Oaks, California: Pine Forge Press.

Ritzer, George (2006): *McDonaldization: The Reader.* Thousand Oaks, California: Pine Forge Press.

Robertson, Susan L. (2005): 'Re-imaging and Rescripting the Future of Education: Global Knowledge Economy Discourses and the Challenge to Education Systems.' In *Comparative Education* 41 (2): pp.151-170.

Robertson, Susan L. (2006a): 'Globalisation, the Rescaling of National Education Systems and Citizenship Regimes.' Public lecture. Bosphorus University, Istanbul, May 17, 2006.

Robertson, Susan L. (2006b): 'Globalisation, Rescaling National Education Systems and Citizenship Regimes.' Centre for Globalisation, Education and Societies, University of Bristol: Mimeo.

Ross, Kenneth N.; Donner-Reichle, Carola; Jung, Ingrid; Wiegelmann, Ulrike, Jürgens-Genevois, Ilona & Paviot, Laura (2006): 'The Main Messages Arising from the Policy Forum.' In Ross, Kenneth N. & Jürgens-Genevois, Ilona (eds.), *Cross-national Studies of the Quality of Education: Planning their Design and Managing their Impact.* Paris: International Institute for Educational Planning, UNESCO, pp.279-312.

Rotberg, Iris C. (ed.) (2004): *Balancing Change and Tradition in Global Education Reform. Scarecrow Education.* Maryland: The Rowman & Littlefield Publishing Group, Inc.

Rubner, Joanne (2006): 'How can a Country Manage the Impact of 'Poor' Cross-national Research Results? A case study from Germany.' In Ross, Kenneth N. & Jürgens-Genevois, Ilona (eds.), *Cross-national Studies of the Quality of Education: Planning their Design and Managing their Impact.* Paris: International Institute for Educational Planning, UNESCO, pp.255-264.

Rust, Val D. (2003): 'Editorial. Method and Methodology in Comparative Education.' In *Comparative Education Review* 47 (3): pp.iii-vii.

Sadler, M.E. (1900): 'How Far can We Learn Anything of Practical Value from the Study of Foreign Systems of Education?' Reprinted (1964), Bereday, George Z.F. & Sadler, Sir Michael (eds.). In *Comparative Education Review* 7 (3): pp.307-314.

Schleicher, Andreas (2005): *A Cross-National Perspective on Some Characteristics Shared by the Best-performing Countries in PISA.* Education Policy Studies Series. The Hong Institute of Educational Research. Hong Kong: The Chinese University of Hong Kong.

Schleicher, Andreas (2006a): 'The Economics of Knowledge: Why Education is Key for Europe's Success.' Brussels, Belgium: The Lisbon Council, Policy Brief.

Schleicher, Andreas (2006b): 'How can International Organizations Work with the Media to Manage the Results of Cross-national Studies? A Case Study from the OECD.' In Ross, Kenneth N. & Jürgens-Genevois, Ilona (eds.), *Cross-national Studies of the Quality of Education: Planning their Design and Managing their Impact.* Paris: International Institute for Educational Planning, UNESCO, pp.265-276.

Schriewer, Jürgen & Martínez, Carlos (2004): 'Constructions of Internationality in Education.' In Steiner-Khamsi, Gita (ed.), *The Global Politics of Educational Borrowing and Lending*. New York: Teachers College Columbia University Press, pp.29-53.

Schriewer, Jürgen (1992): 'The Method of Comparison and the Need for Externalization: Methodological Criteria and Sociological Concepts.' In Schriewer, Jürgen & Holmes, Brian (eds.), *Theories and Methods in Comparative Education*. 3rd edition. Frankfurt am Main; Bern; New York; Paris: Peter Lang Publishing.

Scott, Janelle T. (2005): 'The Context of School Choice and Student Diversity.' Introduction. In Scott, Janelle T. (ed.), *School Choice and Diversity: What Evidence Says*. New York: Teachers College Press.

Simola, Hannu (2005): 'The Finnish Miracle of PISA: Historical and Sociological Remarks on Teaching and Teacher education.' In *Comparative Education* 41 (4): pp.455-470.

Soudien, Crain (2005): 'Globalisation and its Malcontents: In Pursuit of the Promise of Education.' In *Asia Pacific Journal of Education* 25 (2): pp.145-158.

Spillane, James P. (2004): *Standard Deviation: How Schools Misunderstand Education Policy*. Cambridge, Massachusetts: Harvard University Press.

Steiner-Khamsi, Gita (2003): 'The Politics of League Tables.' In *Online Journal for Social Science Education*. 1-2003: 1-6. Retrieved on May 9, 2006 from http://www.sowi-onlinejournal.de/2003-1/tables_khamsi.htm.

Steiner-Khamsi, Gita (ed.) (2004): *The Global Politics of Educational Borrowing and Lending*. New York: Teachers College Columbia University Press.

Steiner-Khamsi, Gita & Stolpe, Ines (2004): 'Decentralization- and Recentralization Reform in Mongolia: Tracing the Swing of the Pendulum.' In *Comparative Education* 40 (1): pp.29-53.

Stoll, Louise & Mortimore, Peter (1997): 'School Effectiveness and School Improvement.' In Barber, Michael & White, John (eds), *Perspectives on School Effectiveness and School Improvement*. London: Institute of Education, University of London.

Stromquist, Nelly P. (2002a): *Education in a Globalized World: The Connectivity of Economic Power, Technology, and Knowledge*. Lanham, Maryland: Rowman & Littlefield Publishers.

Stromquist, Nelly P. (2002b): 'Preface.' In *Comparative Education Review* 46 (1): pp.iii-viii.

Stromquist, Nelly P. (2002c): 'Globalization, the I, and the Other.' In *Current Issues in Comparative Education* 4 (2): pp.87-94.

Stromquist, Nelly P. (2005): 'Comparative and International education: A Journey Toward Equality and Equity: *Harvard Educational Review* 75 (1): pp.89-111.

Tatto, Maria Teresa (1999) 'Education Reform and State Power in Mexico: The Paradoxes of Decentralization.' In *Comparative Education Review* 43 (3): pp.251-282.

Theisen, Gary L.; Achola, Paul P.W. & Boakari, Francis Musa (1986): 'The Underachievement of Cross-national Studies of Achievement.' In

Altbach, Philip G. & Kelly, Gail P. (eds.), *New Approaches to Comparative Education*. Chicago: The University of Chicago Press.

Thut, I.N. & Adams, Don (1964): *Educational Patterns in Contemporary Societies*. New York: McGraw-Hill Series in Education.

Torres, Rosa-María (2003): 'Improving the Quality of Basic Education? The Strategies of the World Bank.' In Beauchamp, Edward R. (ed.), *Comparative Education Reader*. New York: Routledge Falmer, Taylor & Francis Books, pp.299-328.

Torres, Carlos Alberto (2002): 'The State, Privatisation and Educational Policy: A Critique of Neo-liberalism in Latin America and Some Ethical and Political Implications.' In *Comparative Education* 38 (4): pp.365-385.

United Nations Educational, Scientific and Cultural Organization (1998): *Laboratorio Latinoamericano de Evaluación de la Calidad de la Educación: Primer Estudio Internacional Comparativo sobre Lenguaje, Matemática y Factores Asociados en Tercero y Cuarto Grado de la Educación Básica*. Primer informe. Retrieved in June 2003 from http://www.unesco.cl/09html/pdf/programa/infLab1.pdf.

United Nations Educational, Scientific and Cultural Organization (2000): *Laboratorio Latinoamericano de Evaluación de la Calidad de la Educación: Primer Estudio Internacional Comparativo sobre Lenguaje, Matemática y Factores Asociados en Tercero y Cuarto Grado de la Educación Básica*. Segundo informe. Retrieved in June 2003 from http://www.unesco.cl/og.htm/pdf/programa/inflab2.pdf.

Välijärvi, Jouni; Linnakylä, Pirjo; Kupari, Pekka; Reinikainen, Pasi & Arffman, Inga (2002): *The Finnish Success in PISA – And Some Reasons Behind It: PISA 2000*. Institute for Educational Research, University of Jyväskylä. Jyväskylä, Finland: Kyrjapaino Oma Oy. Retrieved on July 15, 2006 from: http://www.jyu.fi/ktl/pisa/base.htm.

van Amelsvoort, H.W.C.H (Gonnie) & Scheerens, Jaap (1997): 'Policy Issues Surrounding Processes of Centralization and Decentralization in European Education Systems.' In *Educational Research and Evaluation* 3 (4): pp.340-363.

van Haecht, Anne (2001): 'Educational Policies: An Exemplary Illustration of Public Policies?' In *European Education* 33 (2): pp.51-73.

van Langen, Annemarie & Dekkers, Hetty (2001): 'Decentralisation and Combating Education Exclusion.' In *Comparative Education* 37 (3): pp.367-384.

Watson, James L. (2004): 'Globalization in Asia: Anthropological Perspectives.' In Suárez-Orozco, Marcelo M. & Qin-Hilliard, Desirée Baolian (eds), *Globalization: Culture and Education in the New Millennium*. Berkeley and Los Angeles, California: University of California Press, pp.141-172.

Watson, Keith (1996): Editorial: *International Journal of Educational Development*. 16 (3): pp.213-214.

Watson, Keith (2000): 'Globalisation, Educational Reform and Language Policy in Transitional Societies.' In Mebrahtu, Teame: Crossley, Michael & Johnson, David (eds.), *Globalisation, Educational Transformation and Societies in Transition*. Oxford: Symposium Books.

Williamson, John (1993): 'Democracy and the "Washington Consensus." ' In *World Development* 23 (8): pp.1329-1336.

Wolhuter, C.C. (1997): 'Classification of National Education Systems: A Multivariate Approach.' In *Comparative Education Review* 41 (2): pp.161-177.

World Bank (1995): *Priorities and Strategies for Education: A World Bank Review. Development in Practice.* Washington DC: The World Bank. http://siteresources.worldbank.org/EDUCATION/Resources/278200-1099079877269/547664-1099080118171/Priorities_and_Strategies_for_Ed_WB_Review.pdf . Retrieved on May 12, 2006.

World Bank (1999a): 'Education Sector Strategy.' Human Development Network Series. Washington DC: The World Bank. http://siteresources. worldbank.org/EDUCATION/Resources/ESSU/education_strategy_1999.pdf. Retrieved on May 12, 2006.

World Bank (1999b) 'Educational Change in Latin America and the Caribbean: Social and Human Development.' Human Development Network Series. Retrieved on May 19, 2006 from http://www-wds.worldbank.org/ external/default/WDSContentServer/IW3P/IB/2000/04/24/000094946_00 041205301922/Rendered/PDF/multi_page.pdf.

World Bank (2004a): 'Education in Indonesia: Managing the Transition to Decentralization.' Report No. 29506. Retrieved on May 12, 2006 from http://siteresources.worldbank.org/EDUCATION/Resources/278200-1099079877269/547664-1099080026826/Edu_Indonesia.pdf.

World Bank (2004b): *World Development Report.* Washington DC: World Bank.

Zedillo Ponce de León, Ernesto (1992): 'Acuerdo Nacional para la Modernización de la Educación Básica (ANMEB)' [National Understanding for the Modernization of Compulsory Education]. In *Diario Oficial de la Federacion (DOF) [Official Federal Register]* May 19, 1992. Retrieved on March 1, 2006 from www.sep.gob.mx.

Zymek, Bernd & Zymek, Robert (2004): 'Traditional – National – International: Explaining the Inconsistency of Educational Borrowers. In Phillips, David & Ochs, Kimberly (eds.), *Educational Policy Borrowing: Historical Perspectives.* Oxford: Oxford Studies in Comparative Education. Symposium Books.

Annex: Total number of observations or people surveyed by country, region and affiliation

Country	Teachers		Principals		Experts			Total
	Public	Private	Public	Private	Academic	Government	International	Interviews
Finland	15	4	8	2	2	2	–	33
Sweden	10	4	8	1	2	5	–	30
France	6	0	6	0	2	4	–	18
United Kingdom	10	12	5	6	3	4	–	40
ENGLAND	2	9	1	5	1	2	–	20
SCOTLAND	8	3	4	1	2	2	–	20
Ireland	2	4	2	6	3	3	–	20
Belgium	3	11	3	6	2	6	–	31
FLANDERS	2	11	2	6	0	6	–	27
WALLONIA	1	0	1	0	0	0	–	2
BELGIUM	0	0	0	0	2	0	–	2
Czech Republic	9	0	7	0	1	1	–	18
Switzerland	9	0	7	0	2	3	–	21
SWTZ – GERMAN	9	0	6	0	0	2	–	17
SWTZ – FRENCH	0	0	1	0	2	1	–	4
Singapore	0	0	0	0	5	0	–	5
Australia	9	4	6	2	4	6	–	31
NSW	7	2	4	1	0	1	–	15
ACT	2	2	2	1	0	2	–	9
AUSTRALIA	0	0	0	0	4	3	–	7
New Zealand	10	6	6	4	6	3	–	35
Hong Kong	2	4	1	3	6	2	–	18
Korea	11	1	7	1	3	0	–	23
Japan	15	2	7	3	1	1	–	29
United States	20	4	9	2	4	3	–	42
BOSTON	9	2	5	1	2	2	–	21
NEW YORK	11	2	4	1	2	1	–	21
Canada	29	2	18	1	8	6	–	64
QUEBEC	6	0	5	0	2	2	–	15
MONTREAL	9	2	3	1	2	2	–	19
ALBERTA	14	0	9	0	2	2	–	27
BRITISH COLUMBIA	0	0	1	0	2	0	–	3
Mexico	23	6	13	3	1	4	–	50
D.F.	6	2	3	1	0	2	–	14
AGUASCALIENTES	15	4	8	2	1	2	–	32
STATE OF MEXICO	2	0	2	0	0	0	–	4
Chile	11	12	6	6	4	3	–	42
International Experts	–	–	–	–	–	–	15	15
Total Surveys	194	76	119	46	59	56	15	565

CERC Publications

Series: CERC Monographs Series in Comparative and International Education and Development

1. Yoko Yamato (2003): *Education in the Market Place: Hong Kong's International Schools and their Mode of Operation.* ISBN 962-8093-57-6. 117pp. HK$100/US$16.

2. Mark Bray, Ding Xiaohao & Huang Ping (2004): *Reducing the Burden on the Poor: Household Costs of Basic Education in Gansu, China.* ISBN 962-8093-32-0. 67pp. HK$50/US$10. [Also available in Chinese]

3. Maria Manzon (2004): *Building Alliances: Schools, Parents and Communities in Hong Kong and Singapore.* ISBN 962-8093-36-3. 117pp. HK$100/US$16.

4. Mark Bray & Seng Bunly (2005): *Balancing the Books: Household Financing of Basic Education in Cambodia.* ISBN 962-8093-39-8. 113pp. HK$100/US$16.

5. Linda Chisholm, Graeme Bloch & Brahm Fleisch (eds.) (2008): *Education, Growth, Aid and Development: Towards Education for All.* ISBN 962-8093-99-1. 116pp. HK$100/US$16

6. Eduardo Andere (2008): *The Lending Power of PISA: League Tables and Best Practice in International Education.* ISBN 978-988-17852-1-3. 138pp. HK$100/US$16.

Series: Education in Developing Asia

1. Don Adams (2004): *Education and National Development: Priorities, Policies, and Planning.* ISBN 971-561-529-5. 81pp. HK$100/US$12 each or HK$400/US$50 for set of five.

2. David Chapman (2004): *Management and Efficiency in Education: Goals and Strategies.* ISBN 971-561-530-9. 85pp. HK$100/US$12 each or HK$400/US$50 for set of five.

3. Mark Bray (2004): *The Costs and Financing of Education: Trends and Policy Implications.* ISBN 971-561-531-7. 78pp. HK$100/US$12 each or HK$400/US$50 for set of five.

4. W.O. Lee (2004): *Equity and Access to Education: Themes, Tensions, and Policies.* ISBN 971-561-532-5. 101pp. HK$100/US$12 each or HK$400/US$50 for set of five.

5. David Chapman & Don Adams (2004): *The Quality of Education: Dimensions and Strategies.* ISBN 971-561-533-3. 72pp. HK$100/US$12 each or HK$400/US$50 for set of five.

Series: CERC Studies in Comparative Education

1. Mark Bray & W.O. Lee (eds.) (2001): *Education and Political Transition: Themes and Experiences in East Asia*. Second edition. ISBN 962-8093-84-3. 228pp. HK$200/US$32.

2. Mark Bray & W.O. Lee (eds.) (1997): *Education and Political Transition: Implications of Hong Kong's Change of Sovereignty*. ISBN 962-8093-90-8. 169pp. [Out of print]

3. Philip G. Altbach (1998): *Comparative Higher Education: Knowledge, the University, and Development*. ISBN 962-8093-88-6. 312pp. HK$180/US$30.

4. Zhang Weiyuan (1998): *Young People and Careers: A Comparative Study of Careers Guidance in Hong Kong, Shanghai and Edinburgh*. ISBN 962-8093-89-4. 160pp. HK$180/US$30.

5. Harold Noah & Max A. Eckstein (1998): *Doing Comparative Education: Three Decades of Collaboration*. ISBN 962-8093-87-8. 356pp. HK$250/US$38.

6. T. Neville Postlethwaite (1999): *International Studies of Educational Achievement: Methodological Issues*. ISBN 962-8093-86-X. 86pp. HK$100/US$20.

7. Mark Bray & Ramsey Koo (eds.) (2004): *Education and Society in Hong Kong and Macao: Comparative Perspectives on Continuity and Change*. Second edition. ISBN 962-8093-34-7. 323pp. HK$200/US$32.

8. Thomas Clayton (2000): *Education and the Politics of Language: Hegemony and Pragmatism in Cambodia, 1979-1989*. ISBN 962-8093-83-5. 243pp. HK$200/US$32.

9. Gu Mingyuan (2001): *Education in China and Abroad: Perspectives from a Lifetime in Comparative Education*. ISBN 962-8093-70-3. 260pp. HK$200/US$32.

10. William K. Cummings, Maria Teresa Tatto & John Hawkins (eds.) (2001): *Values Education for Dynamic Societies: Individualism or Collectivism*. ISBN 962-8093-71-1. 312pp. HK$200/US$32.

11. Ruth Hayhoe & Julia Pan (eds.) (2001): *Knowledge Across Cultures: A Contribution to Dialogue Among Civilizations*. ISBN 962-8093-73-8. 391pp. HK$250/US$38.

12. Robert A. LeVine (2003): *Childhood Socialization: Comparative Studies of Parenting, Learning and Educational Change*. ISBN 962-8093-61-4. 299pp. HK$200/US$32.

13. Mok Ka-Ho (ed.) (2003): *Centralization and Decentralization: Educational Reforms and Changing Governance in Chinese Societies*. ISBN 962-8093-58-4. 230pp. HK$200/US$32.

14. W.O. Lee, David L. Grossman, Kerry J. Kennedy & Gregory P. Fairbrother (eds.) (2004): *Citizenship Education in Asia and the Pacific: Concepts and Issues*. ISBN 962-8093-59-2. 313pp. HK$200/US$32.

15. Alan Rogers (2004): *Non-formal Education: Flexible Schooling or Participatory Education?*. ISBN 962-8093-30-4. 306pp. HK$200/US$32.

16. Peter Ninnes & Meeri Hellstén (eds.) (2005): *Internationalizing Higher Education: Critical Explorations of Pedagogy and Policy.* ISBN 962-8093-37-1. 231pp. HK$200/US$32.

17. Ruth Hayhoe (2006): *Portraits of Influential Chinese Educators.* ISBN 10: 962-8093-40-1; ISBN 13: 978-962-8093-40-3. 398pp. HK$250/US$38.

18. Aaron Benavot & Cecilia Braslavsky (eds.) (2006): *School Knowledge in Comparative and Historical Perspective: Changing Curricula in Primary and Secondary Education.* ISBN 10: 962-8093-52-5; ISBN 13: 978-962-8093-52-6. 315pp. HK$200/US$32.

19. Mark Bray, Bob Adamson & Mark Mason (eds.) (2007): *Comparative Education Research: Approaches and Methods.* ISBN 10: 962-8093-53-3; ISBN 13: 978-962-8093-53-3. 444pp. HK$250/US$38

20. Peter D. Hershock, Mark Mason & John N. Hawkins (eds.) (2007): *Changing Education: Leadership, Innovation and Development in a Globalizing Asia Pacific.* ISBN 13: 978-962-8093-54-0. 348pp. HK$200/US$32.

21. Vandra Masemann, Mark Bray & Maria Manzon (eds.) (2007): *Common Interests, Uncommon Goals: Histories of the World Council of Comparative Education Societies and its Members.* ISBN 13: 978-962-8093-10-6. 384pp. HK$250/US$38.

22. David L. Grossman, Wing On Lee & Kerry J. Kennedy (eds.) (2008): *Citizenship Curriculum in Asia and the Pacific.* ISBN: 978-962-8093-69-4. 268pp. HK$200/US$32.

23. Nancy Law, Willem J Pelgrum & Tjeerd Plomp (eds.) (2008): *Pedagogy and ICT Use in Schools around the World: Findings from the IEA SITES 2006 Study.* ISBN 978-962-8093-65-6. 296pp. HK$250/US$38.

24. Donald B. Holsinger & W. James Jacob (eds.) (2008): *Inequality in Education: Comparative and International Perspectives.* ISBN 978-962-8093-14-4. 584pp. HK$300/US$45.

Other books published/distributed by CERC

1. Mark Bray & R. Murray Thomas (eds.) (1998): *Financing of Education in Indonesia.* ISBN 971-561-172-9. 133pp. HK$140/US$20. [Out of print]

2. David A. Watkins & John B. Biggs (eds.) (1996, reprinted 1999): *The Chinese Learner: Cultural, Psychological and Contextual Influences.* ISBN 0-86431-182-6. 285pp. HK$200/US$32.

3. Ruth Hayhoe (1999): *China's Universities 1895-1995: A Century of Cultural Conflict.* ISBN 962-8093-81-9. 299pp. HK$200/US$32. [Out of print]

4. David A. Watkins & John B. Biggs (eds.) (2001): *Teaching the Chinese Learner: Psychological and Pedagogical Perspectives.* ISBN 962-8093-72-X. 306pp. HK$200/US$32.

5. Mark Bray with Roy Butler, Philip Hui, Ora Kwo & Emily Mang (2002): *Higher Education in Macau: Growth and Strategic Development.* ISBN 962-8093-60-6. 127pp. HK$150/US$24.

6. Yoko Yamato & Sally Course (2002): *Guide to International Schools in Hong Kong*. ISBN 962-8093-62-2. 82pp. HK$72/US$12. [Out of print]

7. Ruth Hayhoe (2004): *Full Circle: A Life with Hong Kong and China*. ISBN 962-8093-31-2. 261pp. HK$200/US$32.

8. 貝磊、丁小浩、黃平 (2004):《減輕貧困家庭的負擔: 中國甘肅基礎教育的家庭成本》。ISBN 962-8093-33-9。53pp。HK$50/US$10 [Also available in English]

9. 貝磊、古鼎儀編 (第二版) (2005)。《香港與澳門的教育與社會：從比較角度看延續與變化》。ISBN 957-496-478-7. 318pp. HK$200/US$32. [繁體版]

10. 貝磊、古鼎儀編 (第二版) (2006)。《香港與澳門的教育與社會：從比較角度看延續與變化》。ISBN 7-107-19379-1. 361pp. HK$60/US$10. [簡體版]

Order through bookstores or from:

Comparative Education Research Centre
Faculty of Education
The University of Hong Kong
Pokfulam Road
Hong Kong, China.

Fax: (852) 2517 4737
E-mail: cerc@hkusub.hku.hk
Website: www.hku.hk/cerc

The list prices above are applicable for order from CERC, and include sea mail postage. For air mail postage, please add US$10 for 1 copy, US$18 for 2-3 copies, US$40 for 4-8 copies. For more than 8 copies, please contact us direct.